WBCA's Offensive Basketball Drills

WBCA's Offensive Basketball Drills

Women's Basketball Coaches Association

Human Kinetics

Library of Congress Cataloging-in-Publication Data

WBCA's offensive basketball drills / Women's Basketball Coaches Association.
    p. cm.
   ISBN 0-7360-0167-0
   1. Basketball--Offense. 2. Basketball for women. 3. Basketball--Coaching. I. Title:
Offensive basketball drills. II. Women's Basketball Coaches Association.

GV889.W37 2000
796.323'082--dc21

                                               99-053660

ISBN: 0-7360-0167-0

Acquisitions Editor: Jeff Riley; **Managing Editor:** Coree Schutter; **Assistant Editors :** Susan Hagan and Wendy McLaughlin; **Consultant:** Kelly Hill; **Copyeditor:** Andrew Smith; **Proofreader:** Robert Replinger; **Graphic Designer:** Nancy Rasmus; **Graphic Artist:** Francine Hamerski; **Photo Editor:** Clark Brooks; **Cover Designer:** Jack W. Davis; **Photographer (cover):** © Brian Spurlock/JRP; **Photographer (interior):** Tom Roberts; **Illustrator:** Sharon Smith; **Printer:** Versa Press

Human Kinetics books are available at special discounts for bulk purchase. Special editions or book excerpts can also be created to specification. For details, contact the Special Sales Manager at Human Kinetics.

Printed in the United States of America   10 9 8 7 6 5 4 3 2 1

Human Kinetics
Web site: http://www.humankinetics.com/

United States: Human Kinetics, P.O. Box 5076, Champaign, IL 61825-5076
1-800-747-4457
e-mail: humank@hkusa.com

Canada: Human Kinetics, 475 Devonshire Road Unit 100, Windsor, ON N8Y 2L5
1-800-465-7301 (in Canada only)
e-mail: humank@hkcanada.com

Europe: Human Kinetics, P.O. Box IW14, Leeds LS16 6TR, United Kingdom
+44 (0)113-278 1708
e-mail: humank@hkeurope.com

Australia: Human Kinetics, 57A Price Avenue, Lower Mitcham, South Australia 5062
(08) 82771555
e-mail: liahka@senet.com.au

New Zealand: Human Kinetics, P.O. Box 105-231, Auckland Central
09-523-3462
e-mail: humank@hknewz.com

CONTENTS

⦿ DRILL FINDER

FOREWORD

It's no secret that today's players are stronger and quicker than those who played the game 20 years ago. With that improved athleticism has come a dramatic increase in offensive production. However, two elements remain constant: sound technique and proper execution. A fancy playbook and a sharp-shooting two guard will get you only so far. The key to any offense lies in the players' abilities to execute the skills necessary for putting the ball in the basket.

WBCA's Offensive Basketball Drills is the best collection of skill-specific and team offensive drills available in one resource. The Women's Basketball Coaches Association is grateful to the 35 college coaches who contributed 87 drills to this fine book.

Whether you're a coach or player, you'll find drills that will produce results. Each aspect of an offense—dribbling, passing, shooting, rebounding—is addressed. We even included 14 transition drills, plus 5 drills dedicated entirely to special situations.

The WBCA believes that instructional resources like this drill book, which was developed by WBCA member coaches, serve a valuable function in the coaching profession and the sport of women's basketball. I encourage you to refer to it and use it often.

Theresa Grentz
President, WBCA

INTRODUCTION

Missing a layup. Giving up a second-chance bucket. Turning it over with the game on the line. These mistakes often are the difference between winning and losing.

To minimize these costly mistakes, your players must have the ability to execute the game's basic skills. And the key to developing these fundamentals lies in the repetition of performing drills, drills, and more drills.

This book unlocks the secret to executing like a champion. We have put together nearly 100 of the finest drills from the top coaches in the game today.

In chapter 1, "Movement Drills," you will learn how to develop players who can cut, slash, pivot, explode, and stop on a dime. Everyone handles the ball in today's game, and chapter 2, "Dribbling Drills," provides you with several drills that will help you develop outstanding ball handling skills from all five players on the floor. In chapter 3, "Passing Drills," you'll learn how to develop skillful passers who understand when and where to deliver the pass so it leads to a scoring opportunity.

Chapter 4, "Screening Drills," includes detailed breakdowns and coaching tips for building screening drills into your practices. Once your players develop an uncanny knack for getting open, the drills in chapter 5, "Shooting Drills," ensure they have got the tools to finish the job. They will, however, miss on occasion. When they do, chapter 6, "Rebounding Drills," ensures they will control the boards.

Some teams attack quickly; others alternate their pace to catch their defenders off-guard. Whatever your transition plan, use the information in chapter 7, "Transition Drills," to make sure your players are effective in putting it to action. In chapter 8, "Situational Drills," you will learn how get that bucket when you most need it.

Champion coaches execute. Year in and year out, their players are well schooled in the fundamentals of the game. Incorporate these drills into your practices today. Hang banners tomorrow.

KEY TO DIAGRAMS

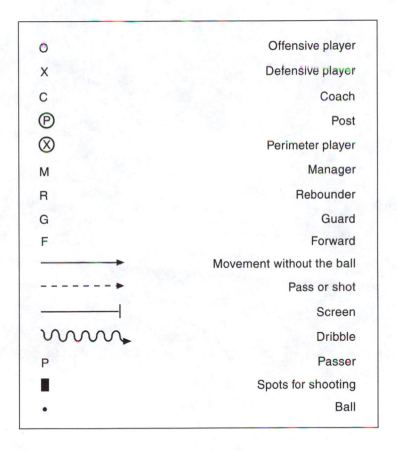

O	Offensive player
X	Defensive player
C	Coach
Ⓟ	Post
Ⓧ	Perimeter player
M	Manager
R	Rebounder
G	Guard
F	Forward
→————→	Movement without the ball
- - - →→	Pass or shot
————⊣	Screen
∿∿∿→	Dribble
P	Passer
▮	Spots for shooting
•	Ball

MOVING DRILLS

Watch any outstanding basketball player and you will notice two common traits: great body balance and control. Lynette Woodard, Teresa Edwards, and Chamique Holdsclaw all exemplify the world-class athlete who balances great speed and agility with strength and quickness. Simply put, they are hard to stop!

A successful player in today's game must have tremendous footwork—either natural or learned—and the ability to cut, slash, pivot, explode, and stop on a dime. Developing sound footwork within the context of game situations and live play is a challenge for any coach. And while most athletes do not relish foot-fire, pivoting, or stopping drills, these are the nuts and bolts that must be mastered to excel in competition in the fast-paced style of today's women's game.

The drills presented in the following section will help you shape your players' enthusiasm for the game and provide them with a framework to develop other skills. Review them often (drill them daily) and your players will react and perform under pressure with amazing grace.

Three-Lane Drill

Coach Pat Summitt
School University of Tennessee

Purpose
To help develop skill in moving without the ball.

Organization
Use three offensive players.

Procedure
1. Players start on the baseline and line up in three lines: on the right side, in the middle, and on the left side of the court, respectively.
2. The ball starts in the middle (see diagram 1).
3. The outside players cut and then come back to the ball.
4. The ball is passed to one side to begin the drill; no dribbling at first.
5. The other two players cut and come back to the ball until they reach the other end of the court.

Coaching Points
- Players must stay in their lane.
- Timing is important. Players must time their cuts and get open when the passer is ready to deliver the pass.

Variations
- Add defensive players (see diagram 2).
- Allow two dribbles to help advance the ball.
- Add a shot at the end of the drill.
- Allow skip passes to the other side of the court.

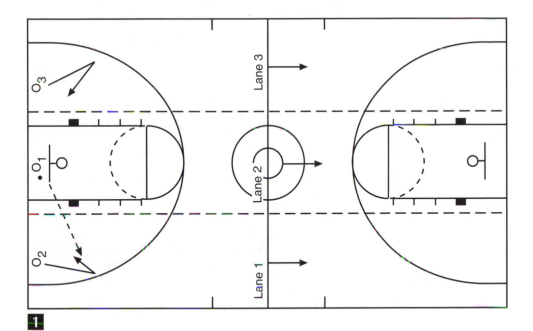

1

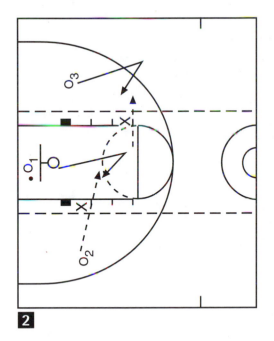

2

Three–Player Cutting Drill

Coach Pat Summitt
School University of Tennessee

Purpose
To cut without the ball and learn to develop proper spacing.

Organization
Use three offensive players.

Procedure
1. Start with the ball at the point with two wing players on either side of the lane at half-court.
2. The point player passes the ball to one of the wings and makes one of the following cuts: give and go, give and go/bump, screen away, or flare (see diagrams 1-4).
3. Once the point player makes a cut, the wing without ball must react accordingly.
4. Continue passing and cutting until a shot is taken.

Coaching Points
- The passer always starts with a pass and cut.
- Players must maintain spacing and continue to react to cutting players.
- Have the players make at least five passes and cuts before shooting.

Variations
- Add a post player to have a post entry.
- Add a defensive post player to challenge passes.

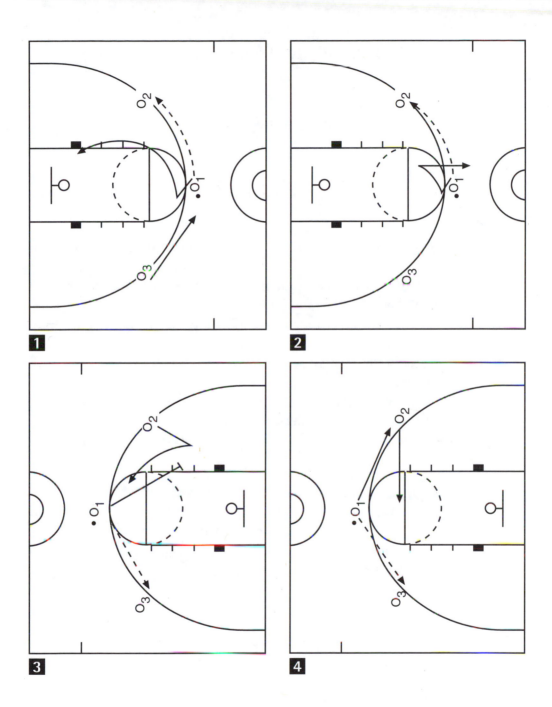

Tag

Coach Chris Gobrecht
School University of Southern California

Purpose
To teach change of speed and direction on offense and attack angles on defense.

Organization
Players work in teams of two (evaders on offense and pursuers on defense).

Procedure
1. Two teams of two step out on the court with one pursuer in each half. Both evaders start along the endline (see diagram 1).
2. The first team of evaders will attempt to get to the opposite endline and evade being tagged by the pursuers.
3. The first evader must cross half-court before the second evader may begin (see diagram 2).
4. The first pursuer must start at the top of the three-point circle and may not pursue beyond half-court.
5. The second pursuer may pursue anyone who has crossed half-court and is not in the *free zone,* the center court circle.
6. Any touch (tag) made on either evader causes both evaders to become pursuers.

Coaching Points
- Players should keep their bodies low with their weight forward. This will help them stay balanced for quick changes of direction.
- Evaders should emphasize acceleration and lateral change of direction.
- Pursuers should emphasize sprinting to position and staying balanced.

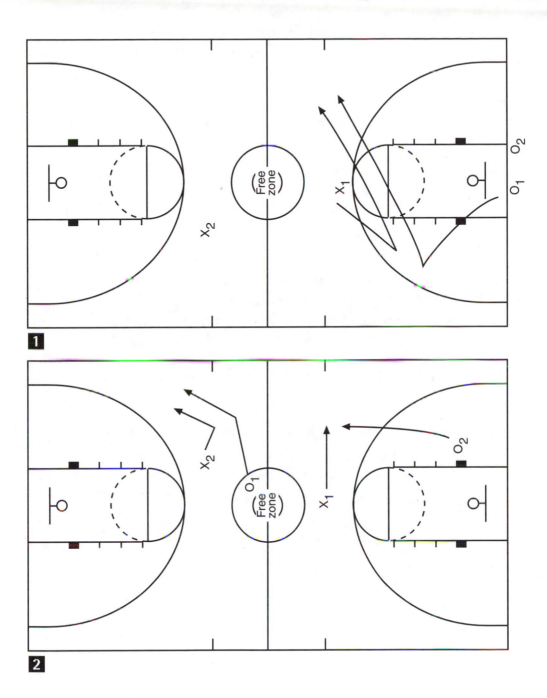

1

2

X-Cut

Coach Trina Patterson
School College of William and Mary

Purpose
To develop movement without the ball on a post entry pass.

Organization
Two lines of perimeter players outside the three-point circle, one along the base line, one outside the three-point circle near the sideline at the free throw line extended; the post player starts on block ballside; balls start in the top line of perimeter players (second cutter line).

Procedure
1. The first cutter line is on the baseline; the second is along the extended free throw line (from sideline to sideline).
2. The second cutter makes a pass into the post player and steps high and away from the baseline (she must wait for the first cutter).
3. Upon passing to the post player, the first cutter cuts toward the baseline and then toward the top side of the post player.

Coaching Points
- The post player may pass to either the cutter or drive herself.
- The second cutter must delay her cut for the first cutter.
- Both cutters must read the post player to see if she will make a move to the basket.

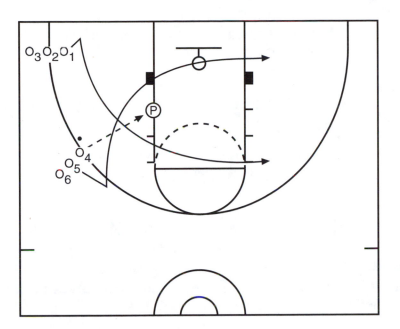

Wrap and Screen

Coach Trina Patterson
School College of William and Mary

Purpose
To develop cutting, change of direction, and screening on the ball.

Organization
Two lines, one for the post players at the top of the key and one for the perimeter players; two balls in the perimeter players' line.

Procedure
1. Each perimeter player makes a pass to the high post player.
2. The perimeter player then makes a hard cut toward the post player (see diagram 1).
3. She wraps around the post player by planting her outside foot to change direction then sets a screen on the post player.
4. The post player will square up and drive to the basket for a layup.

Coaching Points
- Crisp passes to the post player and hard acceleration on the first three strides toward the post.
- Perimeter players must accelerate to position and stay balanced to set a solid screen.

Variation
Send the perimeter player to wrap and go (replace) herself at the wing while the post player squares up to drive or passes back to the perimeter (see diagram 2).

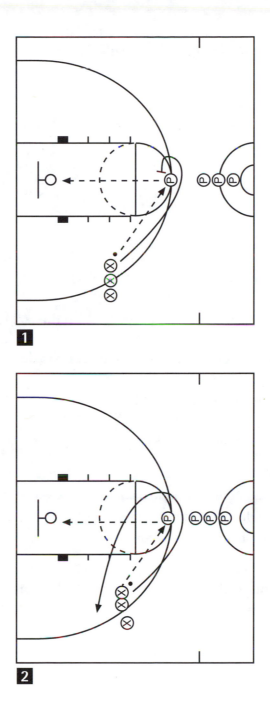

1

2

Basket Cut

Coach Trina Patterson
School College of William and Mary

Purpose
To encourage players to pass and make strong cuts toward the rim without the ball.

Organization
Two passing lines on either side of the court outside the three-point circle; two lines underneath the basket with the first players starting at midpost area.

Procedure
1. Each perimeter player starts with a ball outside the three-point circle (see diagram 1).
2. Perimeter players pass to the post player and then take one step toward the baseline.
3. The perimeter player then makes a hard cut up to the top side of the post player.
4. The post player passes to the perimeter player, who makes a layup.
5. The passer then goes to the end of the baseline.
6. The perimeter player switches lines.

Coaching Points
- Change speed on the cut to the basket.
- Cut hard with the hands in catching position.
- Alternate sides; have space to cut.

Variation
Move perimeter player lines to the baseline for basket cuts on the bottom side of the post (see diagram 2).

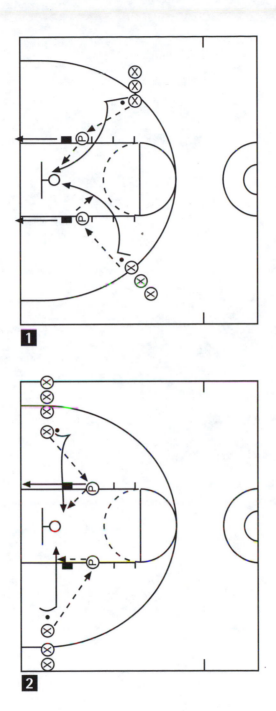

DRIBBLING DRILLS

Everyone handles the ball in today's game. Gone are the days when only the guards were allowed to dribble and posts were forbidden from putting the ball on the floor. Motion offenses require outstanding ballhandling skills from all five players in both half- and full-court situations. And while not every team has a Dawn Staley or Jennifer Azzi to break the press, the more confident and skilled teams can handle most presses with a combination of good court awareness and purposeful dribbling.

Teams that put the ball in their most competent ball handler's hands are wise but are also limited in pressing and trapping situations. As the game changes and bigger players develop the ability and instinct to handle the ball in the open court, defenses are stretched and challenged to try to stop five players from advancing the ball. Improved dribbling has made pressing defenses think twice a time or two.

Build a solid foundation for offensive success with confident and skilled ball handlers—a whole team of them!

Figure–Eight Dribbling

Coach Angie Lee
School University of Iowa

Purpose
To work on handling the ball at different speeds and in varying directions.

Organization
One line at the corner of the court, and everyone has a ball.

Procedure
1. The first player in line speed dribbles to half-court; once at half-court, the next player in line can start.
2. At half-court, the player must reverse pivot and slide dribble across half-court.
3. At the other sideline, the player must backpedal while controlling the ball; at the opposite endline, she must slide dribble across the baseline.
4. At the corner, the player must speed dribble to half-court, reverse dribble, and slide dribble across half-court.
5. At the other side, the player must backpedal while controlling the ball and at the baseline slide dribble to the starting corner.
6. The drill starts over again.

Coaching Points
- Keep head and eyes up at all times.
- Keep dribble below the waist and control the ball.
- Change speeds and accelerate after each change while controlling the ball.

Variation
Compete a certain number of figure eights in a given amount of time or according to a given number of figure eights to be completed.

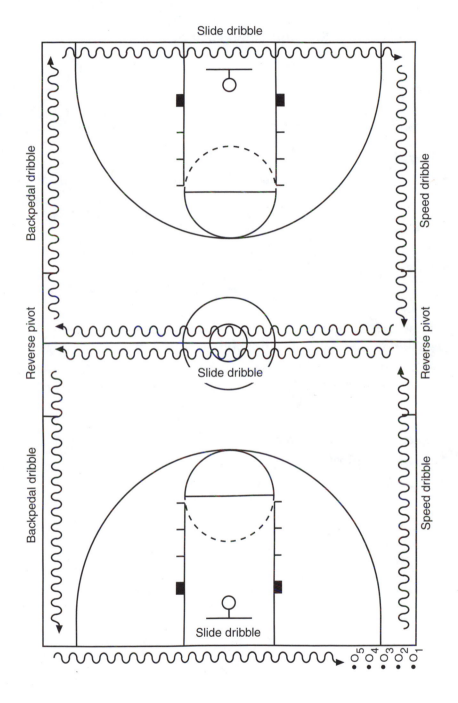

Slide dribble

Backpedal dribble

Speed dribble

Reverse pivot

Reverse pivot

Slide dribble

Backpedal dribble

Speed dribble

Slide dribble

8 | Change Ballhandling

Coach Angie Lee
School University of Iowa

Purpose
To keep the head up while controlling the ball and changing direction quickly on verbal command.

Organization
In partners across from each other, spread out on the floor; everyone has a ball.

Procedure
1. The coach gives a command, such as "start ball in the right hand and on change go between the legs to the left."
2. The coach says "go," and as players approach each other, she or he calls "change."
3. On the change command, the players will dribble the ball between their legs to their left hand, pass each other, and continue dribbling.
4. The coach calls another ballhandling skill, having players start again by facing one another.

Coaching Points
- Listen and keep head and eyes up.
- Dribble in control.
- Accelerate out of "change" call.

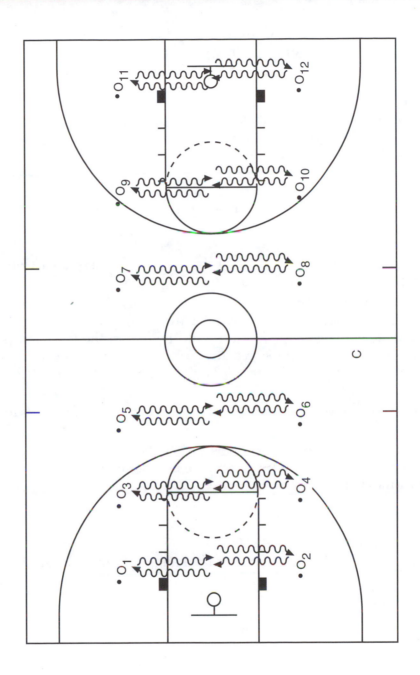

9 Full-Court Ballhandling

Coach Angie Lee
School University of Iowa

Purpose
To handle the ball through a series of different ballhandling changes down the full length of the floor.

Organization
Three lines of three players with extra players along the baseline; three coaches or managers at half-court facing each line.

Procedure
1. The coach calls out the hand he or she wants the players to start with and what he or she wants at each change point.
2. Changes happen at the free throw line, half-court (doing the ballhandling move on the coach), and at the far free throw line, finishing at the opposite endline. *Example:* Start with the ball in the left hand, speed dribble to crossover at the free throw line, control the dribble to reverse dribble at half-court, and dribble behind the back at the other free throw line.
3. The next player in line starts when the player in front of her gets to half-court.
4. As each player comes back, the coach should call a new series of ballhandling skills or tell the player to use the same series starting with the other hand.

Coaching Points
- Listen and keep head and eyes up.
- Control the ball at different speeds, changing from high speed to controlled speed.
- Protect the ball.

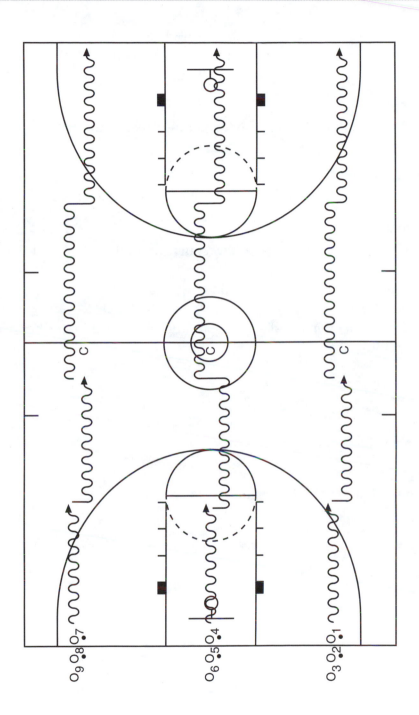

10   Two-Ball Handling

Coach Angie Lee
School University of Iowa

Purpose
To work on handling two balls at once, getting a feel for the ball, and working on dexterity.

Organization
Two or three lines of players on the baseline; every player has two balls.

Procedure
1. Players dribble up and down the court handling two balls at the same time.
2. A coach tells players what to do (e.g., dribble balls at the same time, alternate dribbles).
3. The next player in line does not start until the player before her reaches half-court.

Coaching Points
- Keep head and eyes up.
- Control the balls—crisp dribbles on finger pads.
- Keep dribble below waist.

Variation
Run the drill as a relay or for time.

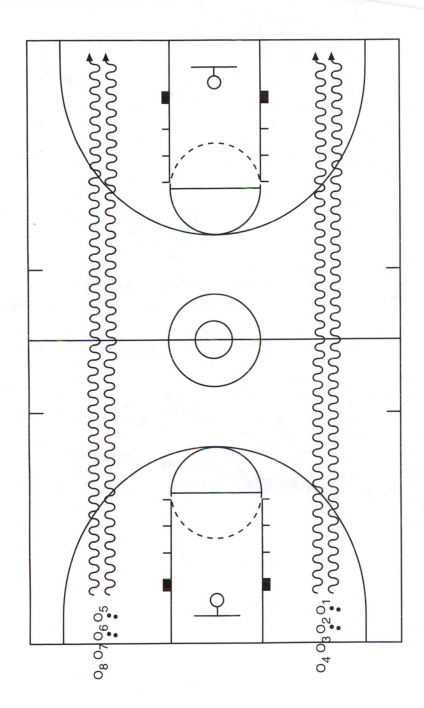

Speed Dribble Chase

Coach Kathy Delaney-Smith
School Harvard University

Purpose
To practice speed dribble and to teach defense to flick ball away from offensive player from behind.

Organization
Players get a partner of similar foot speed. Each set of partners has a ball on the endline.

Procedure
1. The dribbler takes two steps in front of the defensive partner. The dribbler may *not* switch her dribbling hand once she starts.
2. The defensive player tries to beat the dribbler to the other endline or to flick the ball from behind.
3. Have the players switch roles and return from the opposite endline.

Coaching Points
- The dribbler wants to use her lead for advantage.
- The defender tries to overcome the lead with speed or good timing of her defensive flick.

Variation
The coach may adjust the dribbler's lead to make it competitive.

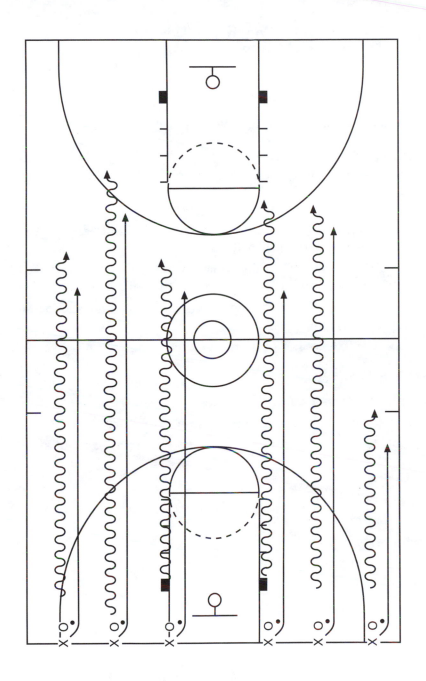

Dribble/Pivot/Pass

Coach Jim Davis
School Clemson University

Purpose

To teach fundamental dribbling, reverse pivots, and chest passing.

Organization

Four lines along baseline; each player in front has a ball.

Procedure

1. The first player in each line executes a big explosive first step and dribbles hard to the free throw line.
2. The player picks up her dribble at the free throw line and tucks it under her chin with her elbows out to protect the ball.
3. The player makes a pivot, steps toward the baseline, and passes to the next player in line.
4. The player follows her pass and returns to the end of the same line.

Coaching Points

- Emphasize taking a strong first step.
- Go down, pick up the dribble, and jump stop on balance.
- Establish and maintain the pivot foot on the reverse pivot and pass.

Variations

- Right front pivot
- Left front pivot
- Right reverse pivot
- Left reverse pivot

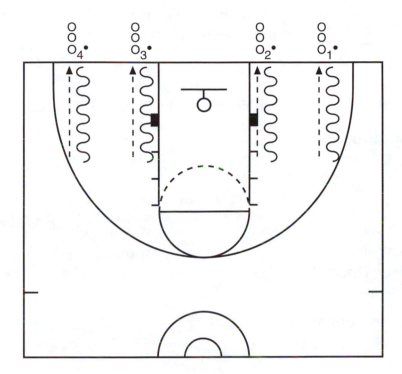

Rooster Fight

Coach Jim Davis
School Clemson University

Purpose
To teach players to protect the ball with the body and to control their dribble.

Organization
All players paired up with someone of similar ability; each player has a ball, and pairs are scattered across the entire floor.

Procedure
1. Each player begins a basic dribble with the dominant hand.
2. Each paired player tries to tip the ball away from her partner.
3. Players change dribbling from the right to the left hand upon the coach's command.

Coaching Points
- Maintain a low and controlled dribble.
- Protect the ball with the body and opposite arm.

Variation
Put players in groups of three (two defenders and one dribbler).

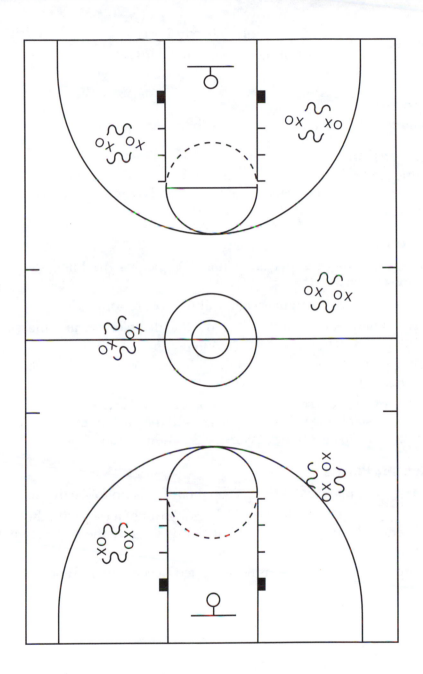

Herding Drill

Coach Wendy Larry
School Old Dominion University

Purpose
To maintain dribble and attempt to dribble out of a trap.

Organization
One line of players at the foul line facing the opposite basket; each person in line has a ball. One line on the right sideline and one on the left sideline, both at half-court.

Procedure
1. The first offensive player in line (O_1) begins dribbling toward the opposite basket.
2. The first defender from each line at half-court approaches the dribbler.
3. Two defenders attempt to "herd" the dribbler toward the sideline where they can trap the ball handler.
4. The player (O_1) must attempt to avoid the trap with her dribble and to score on the two defenders.
5. If the player (O_1) scores or picks up her dribble without a shot or if the defense steals the ball, everyone goes to the back of the line they came from and the next three players begin immediately.

Coaching Points
- Make sure players dribbling keep their heads up to see the floor.
- Teach players to avoid traps by backing out of a trap with the dribble, splitting the trap with the dribble, or driving by the trap before it can be set.
- Emphasize that a player is not expected to beat the trap and score every time.

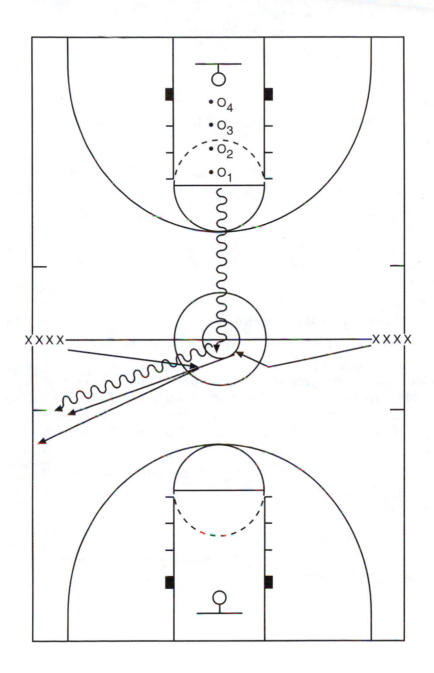

Killer

Coach Rene Portland
School Penn State University

Purpose

To work on players' ballhandling skills while also improving players' defensive skills and stamina.

Organization

Two balls, four players. Players form one line along the baseline.

Procedure

1. The first player in line steps out and becomes the defensive player (X). See diagram 1. The second player has the ball and is the offensive player (O_1).

2. The offensive player attempts to beat the defensive player to half-court using any variety of dribbles.

3. The defensive player attempts to contain the offensive player by forcing her to change direction.

4. Once both players reach half-court, the defensive player sprints back toward the basket. The next player in line (O_2) calls out a shot (layup, elbow, three-pointer) and passes the ball to the former defensive player. The player catches the ball and shoots the shot that was called out. The offensive player (O_1) goes to the end of the line (see diagram 2).

5. After the player (X) shoots, that player plays defense on the next person in line. The defensive player should go three times, executing each shot listed above.

Coaching Point

This is very challenging for the defensive player. They will need plenty of encouragement to survive "killer."

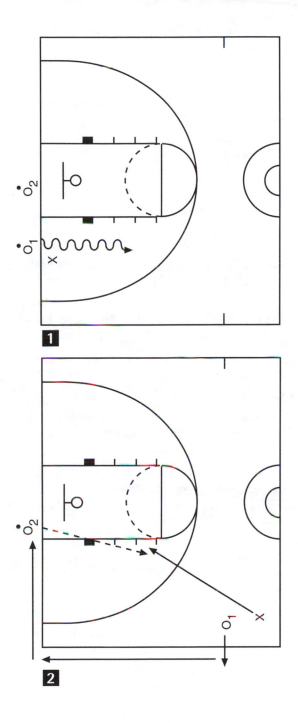

1

2

Sixer Drill

Coach Rene Portland
School Penn State University

Purpose
To develop players' ballhandling skills; also develops skills in reading defense, passing, and penetrating with the ball.

Organization
Three players, one ball, and three lines. Additional players and balls may be used for the drill to run continuously.

Procedure
1. Players form two lines at midcourt. The line closest to the sideline will be on offense. The line closest to the jump circle will be on defense. A third line is needed on the baseline opposite the side of the other two lines.

2. From midcourt, a coach or manager throws the ball toward the sideline in front of the offensive player (see diagram 1).

3. The offensive player receives the ball and goes to the basket to score. The offensive player must read the defense and decide whether to go strong for a layup or pull up for a jump shot.

4. The defensive player leaves as soon as the ball is thrown. She tries to chase and catch the offensive player in order to stop that player from scoring.

5. As soon as the offensive player (O_1) puts up a shot (make or miss), that player retreats down the court on defense. The defensive player then moves to the opposite wing to become the outlet player. The first person in the line along the baseline (O_4) steps onto the court, rebounds the ball, and makes an outlet pass. The drill continues with a two-on-one break in the opposite direction (see diagram 2).

Coaching Points
- For continuous play, the two-on-one break should be carried out on the half of the court opposite of the one-on-one. The two-on-one can then widen once it reaches half-court to use the full half of the court.

- As the two-on-one part of the drill continues, a new set of players can begin the one-on-one part of the drill.

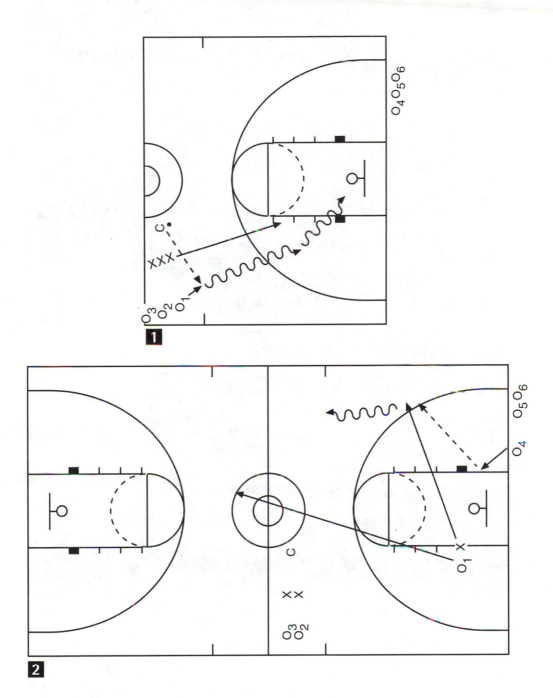

1

2

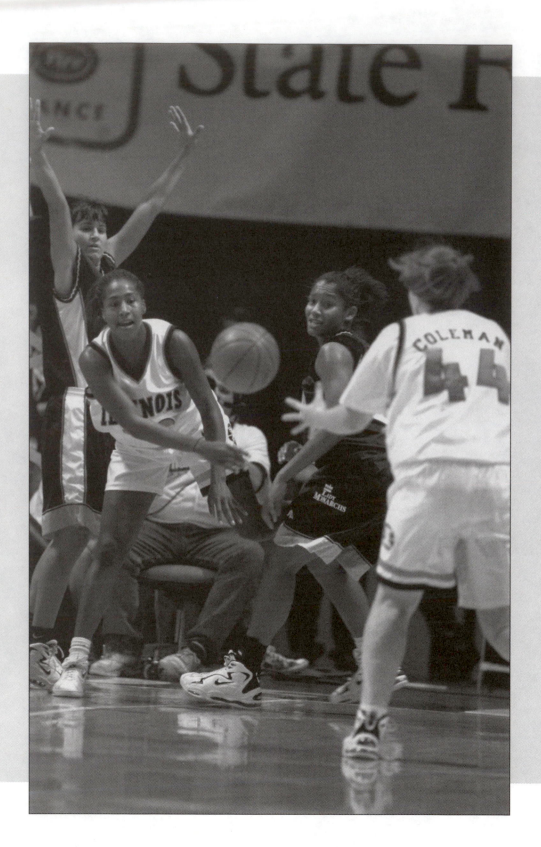

3

PASSING DRILLS

The no-look passes of Stephanie White-McCarty, Nykesha Sales, and Becky Hammon bring the crowds to their feet—and sometimes cause their coaches to squirm in their seats. But the skillful passer understands when and where to deliver a pass so it leads to a scoring opportunity. Teams that drill on passing focus on eye contact, verbal communication, and, of course, timing.

For open-court teams like Stanford, Tennessee, Georgia, and Connecticut, passing in transition is an art form. The eye contact, communication, and accuracy of passing in the open court has put a stamp on the women's game; it is what makes the game so popular. When John Wooden comments that "the best pure basketball I see today is among the better women's teams," what more needs to be said? Great passing is the cornerstone of unselfish team play. It builds confidence in all players and encourages communication. The following drills will help you build each player's confidence and skill so that she can enjoy the thrill of a great assist!

17 Six-Passer Fast Break

Coach Tara VanDerveer
School Stanford University

Purpose
To practice full-court passing, layups, and conditioning.

Organization
Four balls (two at each end of the court) and six passers. Start with one and a half minutes and work up to two minutes on each side. Switch passers and shooters after each side is done.

Procedure
1. At least three shooters start on opposite ends of the court.
2. Each end starts at the same time by passing to the first target (passer)—no dribbles.
3. The shooter continues down the court passing to the next target (passer) on her side without dribbling.
4. The shooter shoots a layup and gets back in line.
5. The drill is continuous.
6. Passers are stationary.

Coaching Points
- No dribbling allowed.
- Provide good targets and sharp passes.
- Sprint the floor and concentrate on finishing layups.
- Switch passes and shooters after time expires.

Variation
Keep track of baskets and make it competitive.

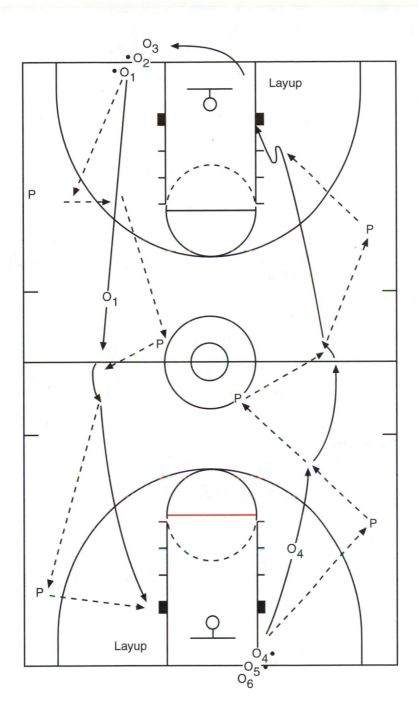

Full-Court Layups

Coach Tara VanDerveer
School Stanford University

Purpose
To develop transition passing skills and conditioning.

Organization
Shooting line on one wing, rebounding line and outlet on opposite side of the court. Two balls are in the shooting line and a rack of balls is at half-court with the coach/passer.

Procedure
1. The first shooter passes across to the first person in the rebounding line then receives the ball back for a layup.
2. The rebounder rebounds and passes to the outlet player (O_6), then the passer (R_1) becomes the outlet player.
3. The outlet player (O_6) passes to the next shooter (O_2) and fills in that line.
4. After the layup, the shooter sprints down the sideline, receives the ball from the coach/passer, scores at the opposite end, and then drives (dribbles up to the ball rack and fills the rebounding line).

Coaching Points
- Sharp passes.
- Concentrate and finish layups on both ends.
- Sprint the floor.

Variation
- You may take away the rack and passer and have the rebounder dribble the full length of the floor for a layup and then dribble back to the shooting line. However, keep in mind you would need every player in the shooting line to have a ball.

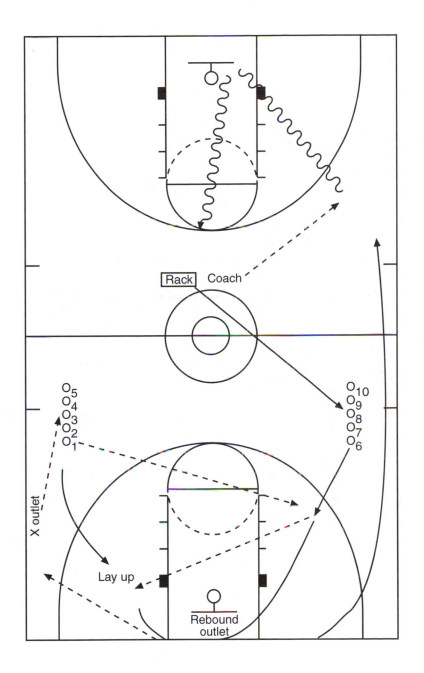

Rack Coach

O_5
O_4
O_3
O_2
O_1

O_{10}
O_9
O_8
O_7
O_6

X outlet

Lay up

Rebound
outlet

19   Three Weave With Trailer

Coach Rene Portland
School Penn State University

Purpose

To improve players' passing skills. This is a good drill for practicing transition up and down the floor as well as improving conditioning.

Organization

One ball, four players. Players divide into four lines along the baseline. Either outside line can be designated as the "trailer" line.

Procedure

1. The first person in the trailer line sprints down the floor. The other three players move down the floor in a weave.

2. Once the trailer reaches the hash mark in the front court, she should cut at a 45-degree angle toward the basket, calling for the ball.

3. Players in the weave may pass the ball no more than three times before hitting the trailer for a layup.

4. The trailer then sprints up the opposite sideline while the same weave continues back down the floor.

5. The trailer must make two consecutive layups before that group can step off the court.

Coaching Points

- The ball may not hit the floor at any time, either from a pass or coming out of the net.

- Passes should be crisp, and players should lead teammates with their passes.

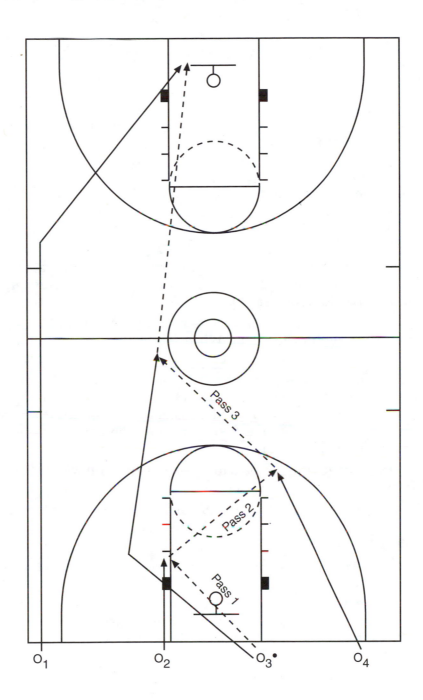

O_1 O_2 O_3• O_4

Pass 1
Pass 2
Pass 3

Rebound, Outlet, Long

Coach Rene Portland
School Penn State University

Purpose

To practice fast-break situations. This is a good drill for improving passing skills and conditioning.

Organization

One ball, three players. Players divide into three lines on the baseline. A coach is needed at either elbow on the far end of the court.

Procedure

1. The ball starts in the middle line. The player with the ball passes to the line opposite of where the coach is to begin the drill (in diagram 1, player O_2 passes to player O_1).

2. Player 1 then passes the ball back to player O_2. Meanwhile, player O_3 sprints the length of the floor. When player O_3 reaches the opposite free throw lane, player O_2 passes the ball to player O_3 for a layup.

3. After completing the pass, player O_2 sprints toward the foul line, circles the coach, and sprints back down the floor. After finishing the layup, player O_3 moves to the outlet position on the opposite side of the floor. Player O_1 sprints the floor, rebounds the ball, and outlets to player O_3 (see diagram 2).

4. Player O_3 then returns the pass to player 1. Player 1 throws a long pass to player O_2 for a layup.

5. The next group takes the ball out of the net and the drill continues.

Coaching Points

- All rebounds should be taken directly out of the net. The ball should not hit the floor.

- Special attention should be paid to the passes in this drill. Long passes should not be thrown directly at the receiver. Instead, they should be thrown ahead of the receiver, thus leading the player into the layup.

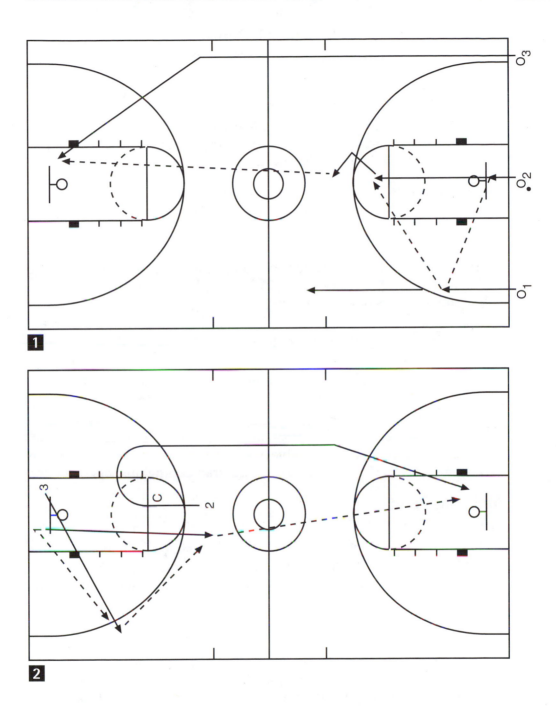

1

2

45

Three-on-Three, Two Bounce

Coach Sue Gunter
School Louisiana State University

Purpose

To work on passing against the pressure of a defender on the ball as well as a defender on the receiver. This drill also allows work both on dribbling and on defense on the ball and the receiver.

Organization

All players in groups of three. Each offensive set of players will have one ball.

Procedure

1. Start this drill at one baseline and complete it at the other baseline. The offensive players are set with one in the middle and one on each sideline. All three players have a defender.

2. The point player (O_2) must stay in the middle third of the court and the wings must stay in their own outer third; each time an offensive player has the ball, she is only allowed two dribbles to advance the ball.

3. This allows the defense to put extreme amounts of pressure on the ball and in the passing lane, putting the defense at a major advantage.

4. Once the ball is put on the floor, the other two offensive players are to sprint up the floor until the second dribble is used. They then must break back toward the ball for a possible pass. In the meantime, the player with the ball must use aggressive, low-weight transfers against her defender.

Coaching Points

- Stress dribbling, passing, and receiving under pressure.

- This is also a good drill to work on ball and passing lane defense in terms of footwork and stance. Beyond that it is a tremendous conditioning drill.

- Stress that a bounce pass, chest pass, or one-handed push pass may be used. The key to the drill is making a solid pass, strong, crisp, and away from the defender, to the receiver under a great amount of pressure.

- This drill is also excellent for teaching players to come back to the ball and to receive the ball under pressure. Passing is only as good as receiving. Once the receiver catches the ball, she transfers the ball low to her outside hand and pushes up the floor for two dribbles, and the drill continues.

Variation

To make the drill more difficult for the offense and to add more intensity to the defense, you can reduce the dribbles allowed from two to one.

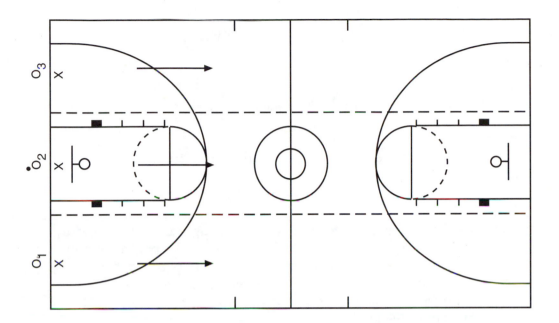

Feed-the-Post Series

Coach Sue Gunter
School Louisiana State University

Purpose
To work on perimeter players feeding the post properly.

Organization
All players work in this drill at one time; two balls in both perimeter lines and two managers with football blocking dummies defending the post players.

Procedure
1. On one side, the perimeter players are lined up on the wing and the manager is defending the post on the high side. The perimeter player drives the ball to be even with the player she wants to feed (pass to) in the low post. With one or two hard dribbles, the perimeter player should be even with the post player and be able to drop a bounce pass into the post away from the defense.

2. In the meantime, the post player should be working on posting and sealing. The key is for her to make contact with her back side against the manager's blocking dummy. For this drill, do not allow the post players to shoot. Have them post, seal, receive, and chin the ball and then look over their shoulder at the basket.

3. On the other side, the perimeter players are lined up in the corner and the manager is defending the post on the low side. The perimeter player should drive the ball toward the wing to feed the post. Again, this is allowing a dribble to improve the passing angle.

4. The post player in this case is working again on posting and sealing. Because the defense is on the low side, the post player would be initiating and sealing down toward the baseline.

5. Perimeter players change sides after each feed but stay on the perimeter. Post players change sides after each feed but stay in the post.

Coaching Points
- The dribble should be hard and quick, followed by a good low pass.
- The bounce pass should be crisp and away from the defense.
- The post player should be sealing with both hands up, calling for the basketball, and stepping to the ball to receive it.

Variation
To make the passer work even more, add a manager as a defender on her.

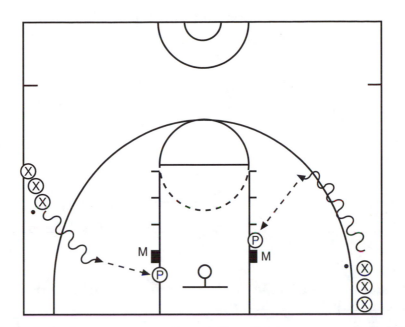

Side-Center-Side

Coach Sue Gunter
School Louisiana State University

Purpose
To work on making crisp, accurate passes while moving up the court.

Organization
The entire team at one time in groups of three. Each group of three will have a ball.

Procedure
1. Place one player in the middle and one player on each side of this player. The two players to either side of the middle player will be between this player and the sideline.
2. All three players move up the court, sprinting as hard as they can and passing the ball back and forth.
3. The ball should never touch the ground, and all passes should be crisp and on target.
4. Have players call out the name of the player they are passing the ball to before each pass. This helps develop communication and recognition.

Coaching Points
- Solid passing while on the move is important in this drill.
- This drill also works on receiving because of the added pressure of catching on the move and then immediately passing the ball back properly.

Variations
- Players can also use bounce passes instead of chest passes.
- Sometimes use a regular ball and at other times use a heavy trainer ball or a medicine ball to develop arm strength.
- Go up and back twice without resting.

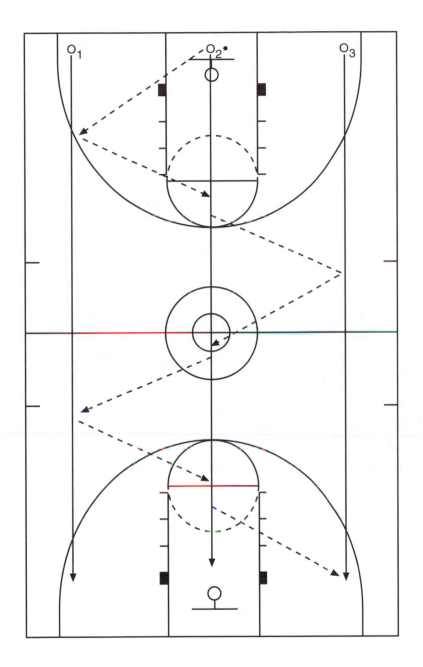

Olympic Passing

Coach Joe McKeown
School George Washington University

Purpose
To improve passing in transition, shooting while on the fast break, filling lanes, and conditioning.

Organization
Three players start at half-court with a ball in the middle; two more players start along baseline each with a ball. Use five balls and seven lines.

Procedure
1. Three players start at half-court.
2. They attack three-on-zero and make a layup.
3. The passer (X_2) and nonshooter (X_1) then receive passes from the baseline passers (O_1) and (O_4) and shoot game shots. The two baseline passers and the layup shooter (X_3) then attack three-on-zero to the other end of court with two baseline passers, making passes to the passer and nonshooter from the second group. This is a continuous drill.

Coaching Points
- Run the lanes hard/hustle.
- Ball should not hit the floor.
- Shoot game shots (e.g., three-pointers, post moves).
- Try to make 30 shots in three minutes.

Variation
Defense can be added.

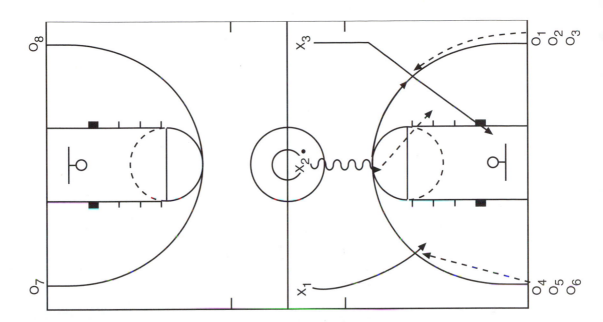

Four-Line Passing Drill

Coach Jody Runge
School University of Oregon

Purpose
To teach strong-hand and weak-hand passing and receiving.

Organization
Four lines each with three players; four balls.

Procedure
1. The first player (O_1) in each line makes a live ball move then dribbles to the free throw line, jump stops, then makes a front or rear turn and a right-handed flick air pass to the next player on the basket.
2. The next player catches the ball with a jump stop and makes a live ball move.
3. The passer (O_1) then changes direction (V-cut, L-cut, or reverse spin) and goes back to the end of the line.
4. The passer then makes a change of direction and goes to the end of the line.

Coaching Points
- Make a live ball move without traveling.
- Jump stop and turn on toe.
- Step into every pass and step to meet every pass.

Variations
- Use a weak-hand pass instead of strong-hand pass.
- Take four dribbles, jump stop, turn, and then make an overhead pass.

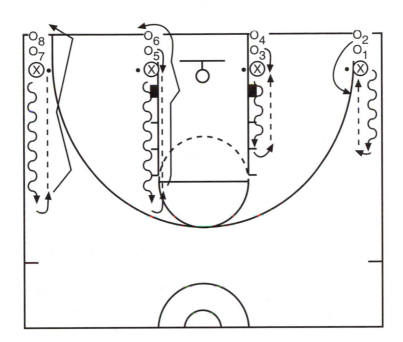

Four-Line Passing Drill With Defense

Coach Jody Runge
School University of Oregon

Purpose

To teach players to pass by a defender.

Organization

Four lines each with four players; four balls.

Procedure

1. The first player in each line spins a pass to herself above the free throw line.
2. The second player in line follows the first player out and defends her.
3. The third player in line posts up and calls for a pass.
4. The offensive player (O_1) must pass by the defender and may dribble to improve the passing lane. Player (O_1) then passes to player (O_3).
5. The offensive and defensive players go to the end of the line, and the next two players depart.

Coaching Points

- The offensive player jump stops, turns, reads the receiver, and passes by the defender.
- The offensive player can dribble to improve the passing angle.

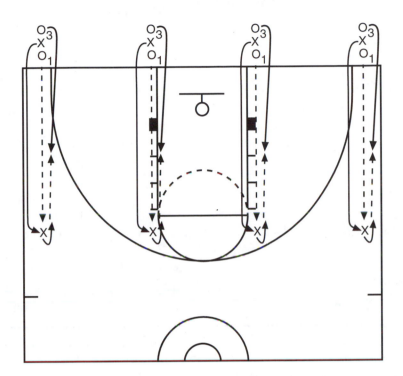

Rush Drill

Coach Kay Yow
School North Carolina State

Purpose
To attempt 25 layups in two minutes. Players can promote good communication skills by calling out each receiver's name during this drill.

Organization
Split the team evenly on each end and form three lines under each end basket. Use four balls.

Procedure
1. The ball begins in the middle line. On a signal the ball is passed from the middle player (B in the diagram) to player A, who is sprinting along the sideline. Player A passes back to player B in the middle. Player B passes ahead to player C, who is sprinting along the other sideline. Player C shoots a layup.

2. Player B, after passing for the layup, sprints to slap the hand of a waiting teammate (O_2) who has one foot on the endline. Player B then sprints to fill the sideline to receive the outlet pass from player A. Player C curls out to the opposite sideline, and player A rebounds and outlets to player B. The drill continues back down in the same manner—pass to the sideline, to the middle, and to the sideline for a layup by player C (see diagram 1).

3. When the first group has shot their first layup and crosses half-court on their return trip, the first three players on that endline (O_1, O_2, and O_3) follow up the court with the same passing pattern—sideline, middle, sideline for a layup. Again, the shooter (O_1) curls out to the sideline opposite the passer (O_2), who has slapped hands with a teammate (E) on that end. The rebounder (O_3) turns this group (O_1, O_2, and O_3) around, and they head back down with sideline, middle, sideline, layup. When they get to half-court, the next group (D, E, and F) begin (see diagram 2).

4. The drill continues for two minutes. The goal is to make 25 layups.

Coaching Points
- Use sharp, quick passes. Give good hand targets.
- All players sprint at game speed.
- Do not walk with the ball. Take a dribble if needed before passing or before shooting the layup.

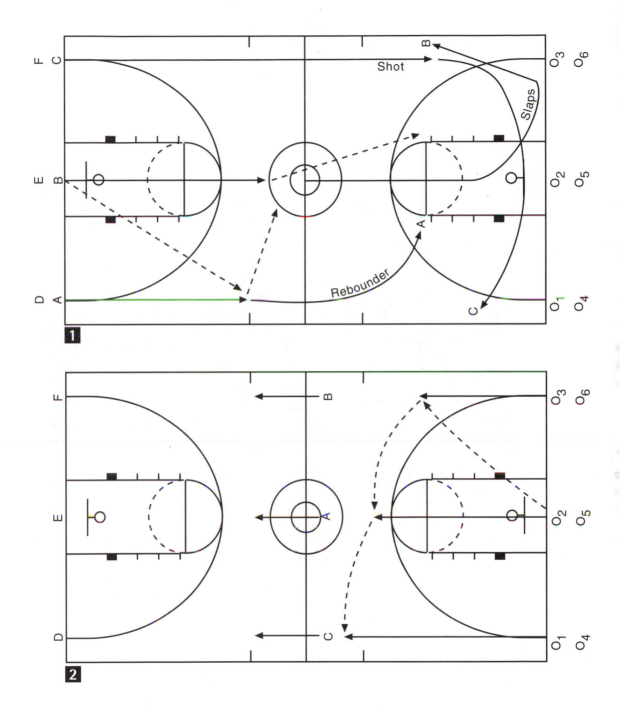

Feed-the-Post Drill

Coach Barbara Stevens
School Bentley College

Purpose

To work on passing skills and reading the defense in a two-on-one or two-on-two situation. To teach conversion outlet passes and getting open under pressure.

Organization

Perimeter players are lined up at midcourt on one sideline. Three to four balls are needed. Post players are lined up under the basket.

Procedure

1. Start two-on-zero. The perimeter player dribbles the ball into the scoring area and feeds the post player, who has positioned herself above the block. The post player works on various post moves to score (see diagram 1).

2. Upon scoring, the post player takes the ball out of the net and throws an outlet pass to the perimeter player, who has run to the opposite sideline for the outlet.

3. The perimeter player dribbles across midcourt and goes to the end of the perimeter line. The post player goes to the end of the post line.

4. The drill continues until all have performed the first segment. Then add defense on the passer. Now the perimeter player dribbles against pressure into the wing area and must execute a successful post feed against the defense.

5. Continue with the post player taking the ball out of the net and throwing an outlet pass to the perimeter player, who is being guarded. She must catch and dribble under pressure to midcourt.

6. The final segment adds a defender on the post player. Now it is a two-on-two drill. Play the shot live and convert offense to defense, playing this way to midcourt.

Coaching Points

- Stress good post feeds.
- The post players work on sealing techniques and post moves.
- Teach the importance of utilizing fakes and change of direction to get open under pressure ("fake a pass to make a pass"), and also stress quick outlets.

Variations

- Add any other two-on-two situation you wish to this drill: pick and roll, pass and cut, etc.
- Add a coach as an open passer to form a ballside triangle to work on angles of feeding the post player (see diagram 2).
- Work both sides of the floor.

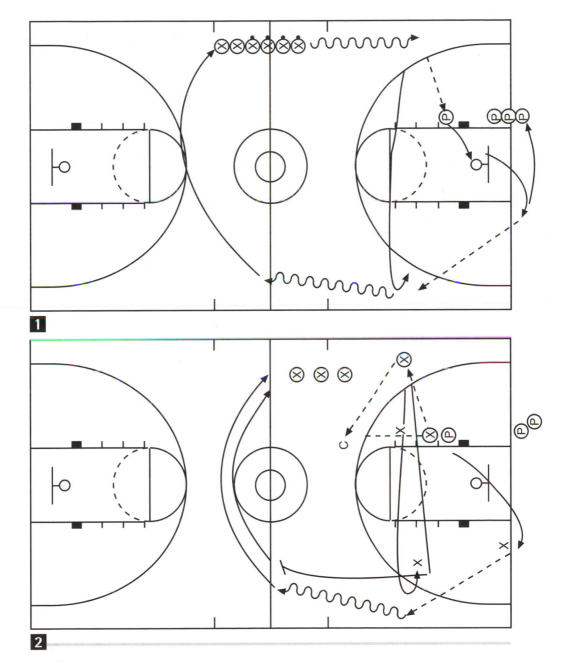

Kentucky Passing Drill

Coach Bernadette Mattox
School University of Kentucky

Purpose
To improve players' passing, cutting, and communication.

Organization
Use at least nine players spread into three lines; each player on the baseline has a ball.

Procedure
1. The first player dribbles up the sideline with her outside hand.
2. The second player (O_4) steps in to receive the pass from the first player then immediately passes to player (O_7).
3. Player (O_7) passes to the second player (O_4), who cuts to the basket for a layup or jumper.
4. The first player (O_1) goes to the second line, the second player (O_4) goes to the third line, and the third player (O7) rebounds and goes to the first line.

Coaching Points
- Crisp passes.
- Call for the ball.
- Meet the pass.
- Give targets.

Variation
Go on both sides.

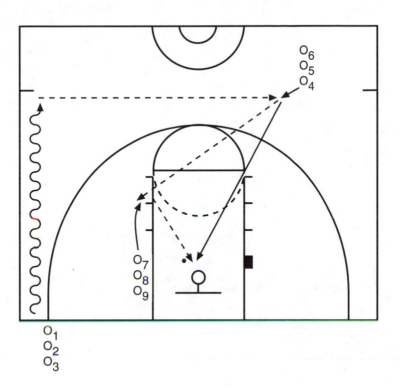

4

SCREENING DRILLS

With few exceptions in today's game, player's do not just "get open"; they have to work to earn their shots. Motion offenses rely heavily on excellent screening execution and getting the ball to their scorers in scoring position.

Stanford could not stop Harvard—or their best player, Allison Feaster—in what was mostly a clinic on screening in the 1998 NCAA Regionals. And who can forget the performance by Sheryl Swoopes in the 1993 NCAA Championships: 16 field goals in a single game! But neither of these great performances would have been possible without their teammates' screens.

In this chapter you'll get some great breakdowns from top coaches and excellent teaching tips on how to build screening drills into your live competitive action. Maybe you do not have the great one-on-one player to create a scoring opportunity for herself, but you can develop a solid basis for all players to work for opportunities through effective screens!

Basic Screen Drill

Coach Kay Yow
School North Carolina State

Purpose
To teach players proper stance and body positioning for screening.

Organization
Split the team into three lines on the endline.

Procedure
1. On a whistle the first three players sprint to the free throw lane, pop their feet on a jump stop with their knees flexed, bodies low, and arms crossed tightly over their chests in a screening stance. They should maintain good balance until the whistle sounds to continue.

2. At the next whistle the first three players sprint to half-court and screen again while the next three in line sprint to the free throw lane and screen.

3. The drill continues until all players have executed a proper screening stance in both free throw lanes and in the center court circle.

Coaching Point
Players must remain low and have good balance, arms crossed, and head and eyes up.

Variation
Have the screeners perform a roll, a step back, or a step to after each screen.

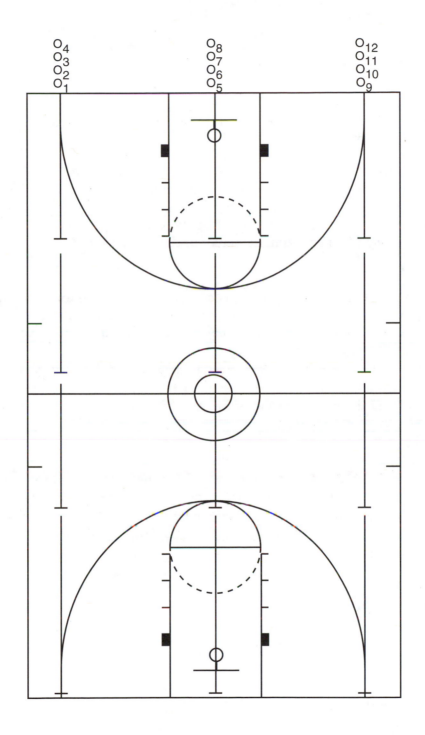

Curl/Flare Drill

Coach Kay Yow
School North Carolina State

Purpose
To teach players the techniques of reading and using a downscreen for a curl cut, a flare, or a backdoor cut.

Organization
One ball for the entire team, a manager/defender, and a passer/coach. Split players into three lines, one at the top of the key, one on one wing, and a third under the basket. The passer/coach begins on the opposite wing with the ball. The defender begins on the player under the basket.

Procedure
1. The drill begins as the passer/coach passes up to the top. The player under the basket cuts out and prepares to use a downscreen on her defender from the wing. The player using the screen must watch her defender reading her defender's position.

2. If her defender trails behind her or is caught by the screen, the offensive player will accelerate at the point of the screen and curl around it, receiving the pass from the passer and scoring (see diagram 1).

3. If her defender goes behind the screen, the offensive player should stop, cut out from the screen, and flare back. The screener will need to pivot and rescreen. The passer will throw an overhead pass to the flaring offensive player. An open shot or quick penetration should result (see diagram 2). (If the defender hustles around the screen before the pass is made, the offensive player should cut backdoor for a pass from the top.)

4. After the first three players execute, the next three step up. The defender remains the same. Player rotation is from under the basket to the wing, from the wing to the top, and from the top to under the basket.

Coaching Points
- The player using the screen for a flare should push off her teammate with both hands in the small of the back, looking for a possible rescreen.
- Cut off the screen shoulder to shoulder and curl tightly around it.
- Walk or jog to set the defender up to use the screen, then accelerate at the point of the screen.
- The screener can either screen an area or a player. When screening an area, set the screen approximately half the distance between the ball and the player to be screened.

Variation

It is especially helpful when first teaching this concept to instruct the defender where to go on the screen. *Example:* have the defender go behind or under the screen consecutively before changing.

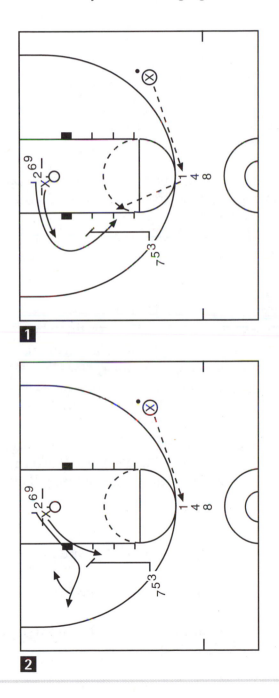

Two-Player Screening and Shooting Drill

Coach Kay Yow
School North Carolina State

Purpose

To teach players the techniques of reading and using screens to cut high for a shot, to curl close for a layup, or to fake using the screen and cut backdoor.

Organization

The entire team with a passer and one ball.

Procedure

1. Split players into two lines, one line at the top of the key with the other line on either wing. A passer/coach should position herself or himself on the wing opposite the line of players.

2. The first player in the middle line starts with the ball; she passes to the coach, steps toward the pass, and then screens away for the first player on the wing (see diagram 1).

3. While the second pass is being made, the wing player steps toward the baseline (setting up her defender) and cuts off the screen for a jump shot. The screener rolls to the basket for the rebound.

4. The drill continues with the next two players in line.

5. The next series has the same alignment. This time the player using the screen cuts to the basket for a layup. The screener steps back away from the cutter. The coach can hit either the cutter to the basket or the screener stepping out (see diagram 2).

6. The last series in the set has the player using the screen to fake up as if cutting by the screen but then cutting to the basket on a backdoor cut. The screener reads that cut and steps to the ball (see diagram 3). The coach can hit either player.

Coaching Points

- Remind players using the screen to set their defenders up by stepping away from the screen first.

- Always accelerate at the point of the screen. Cut shoulder to shoulder on the curl cut.

- Screeners should position themselves in a balanced stance and keep their knees flexed, especially as they move to roll.

Variations

- Run the drill to both sides of the floor.
- Add defense on both lines.

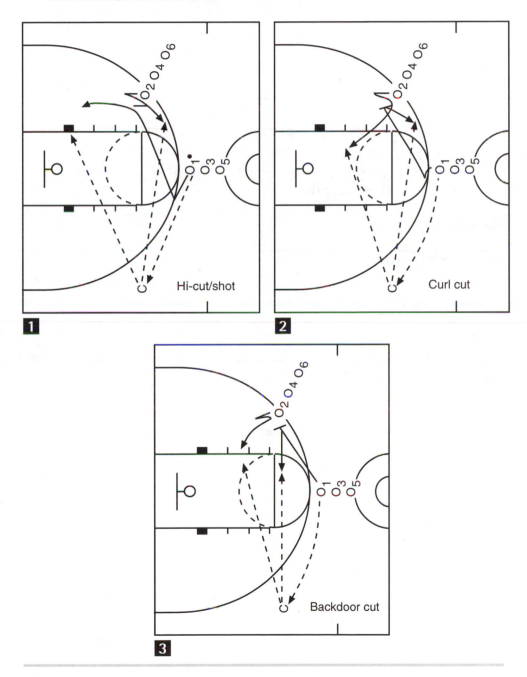

Hi-cut/shot

1

Curl cut

2

Backdoor cut

3

Downscreen

Coach Carol Ross
School University of Florida

Purpose
To teach proper technique for setting a downscreen.

Organization
Minimum three players with one ball.

Procedure
1. A coach starts with the ball at the top.
2. One player starts on the wing and one player starts on the block.
3. The first player sets a downscreen for the second player on the block.
4. The second player should set up her cut and use the screen. She should look to score after using the screen.
5. The first player should open up and roll to the ball after contact has been made.

Coaching Points
- On a downscreen, the screener's back should angle away from the basket.
- The screener must stay low and maintain a wide, strong base.
- The screener should always open up (roll) to the ball after contact has been made so that she is a threat to score (especially important against a switching defense).

Variation
Add defenders and build up to two-on-two; also, you may sometimes allow only the screener (O_1) to score.

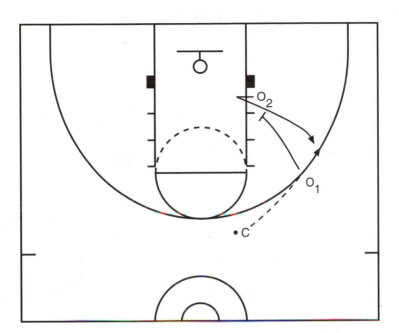

Backscreen

Coach Carol Ross
School University of Florida

Purpose
To teach proper technique for setting a backscreen.

Organization
Minimum three players or a coach and two players with one ball.

Procedure
1. The coach starts with the ball at the top.
2. One player starts on the wing and one starts on the block.
3. The player on the block sets a backscreen for the wing player.
4. The wing player should set up her cut and use the screen. She should look to score after using the screen and receiving a pass from the coach.
5. The player on the block should step (roll) toward the ball after contact has been made on the screen.

Coaching Points
- On a backscreen, the screener's back should angle toward the basket.
- The screener must stay low and maintain a wide, strong base.
- The screener should always step (roll) toward the ball after contact has been made so that she is a threat to score (especially important against a switching defense).

Variation
Add defenders and build up to two-on-two.

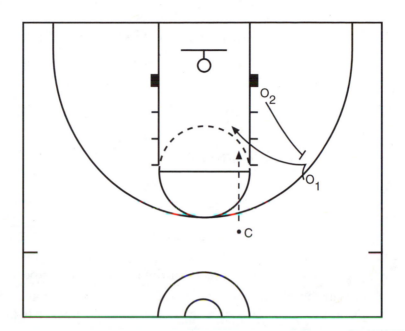

Read the Defense

Coach Carol Ross
School University of Florida

Purpose
To teach players how to read the defense and use the downscreen.

Organization
Minimum three players with one ball.

Procedure
1. A coach starts with the ball at the top.
2. One player starts on the block with a defender and one player starts on the wing without defense.
3. The wing player sets a downscreen for the player on the block.
4. The player on the block reads the defense, sets up her defender, and makes the appropriate cut—pop up, curl, flair, or back cut (see diagrams 1-4).

Coaching Points
- A pop-up cut is used if the defender runs directly into the screen.
- A curl cut is used if the defender is trailing or gets caught trying to get over the top of the screen.
- A flair cut is used if the defender tries to go behind the screen and beat the cutter to her spot.
- A back cut is used if the defender cheats up higher than the screen.
- The cutter must watch her defender, not the ball, when trying to determine which cut to make.

Variation
Add defenders and build up to two-on-two.

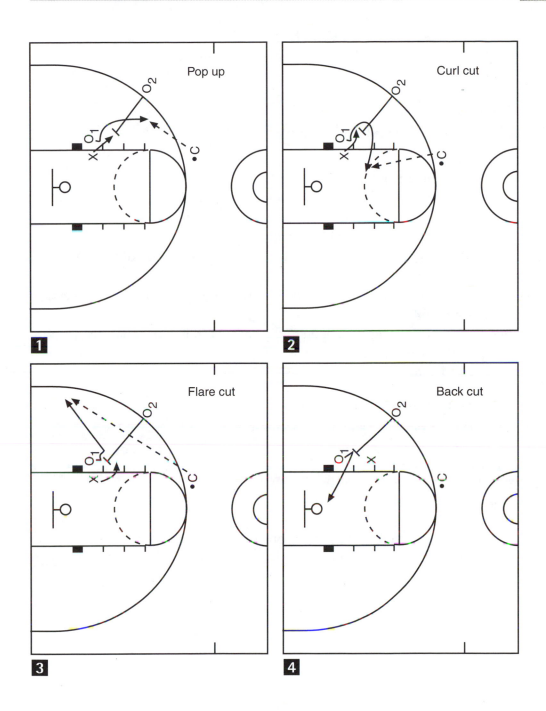

Pick and Roll

Coach Carol Ross
School University of Florida

Purpose
To teach proper technique for setting a screen on the ball.

Organization
Minimum three players with one ball.

Procedure
1. The first player starts on the wing with the ball.
2. The second player starts on a ballside block and steps out to set a screen on the ball.
3. The first player sets up her defender by jabbing opposite of the direction she's going.
4. The second player rolls open to the basket after contact has been made.
5. The first player comes off the screen looking to score or pass to the second player.

Coaching Points
- The screener must stay low and maintain a wide, strong base.
- The screener must remain stationary until contact is made.
- The screener rolls to the basket after contact is made, calls for the ball, and shows the ball handler a big target.

Variations
The ball handler can start anywhere on the perimeter, and the screen can also come from different positions; add defenders and build up to two-on-two.

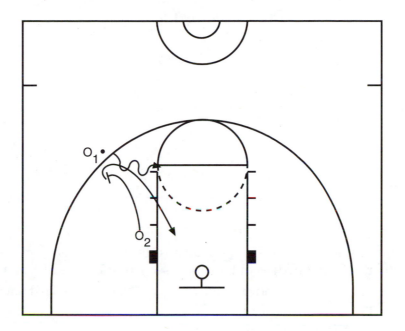

Slip Screen

Coach Gordy Presnell
School Seattle Pacific University

Purpose
To create a pressure release when the opponent doubleteams or hedges out early on the pick and roll.

Organization
Four players: two offensive, two defensive; one ball.

Procedure:
1. The players set above the key in a two-guard front set.
2. An offensive player (O_2) begins to set an offense screen on defender (X_1); another defender hedges out to stop a second offensive player (O_1).
3. O_1 sees the second defender hedge and gives O_2 the closed fist (backdoor cut) sign.
4. O_2, seeing the fist, immediately dive cuts toward the basket, receiving the pass from O_1.

Coaching Points
- O_2 must sell the screen before effectively slipping it.
- O_1 must read the defense and be prepared for a quick-hitting pass to O_2.

Variation
Defenders modify their positions so that O_1 and O_2 can read the defense and cut accordingly.

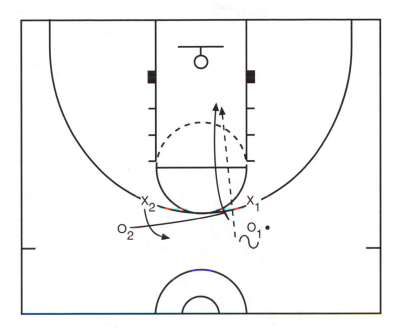

Backscreen Roll

Coach Gordy Presnell
School Seattle Pacific University

Purpose
To motivate the screener to be more offensively minded.

Organization
Two players with one ball. The coach acts as a passer on the wing.

Procedure
1. One offensive player (O_2) begins on the weak side. Player (O_1) initiates the drill from the top of the key.
2. O_1 passes to the coach, and O_2 sets a backscreen on O_1's defender.
3. O_1 fades off the screen, preparing for a skip pass from the coach.
4. O_2 rolls to the ball.
5. The coach passes to O_1 or O_2 for a shot attempt.

Coaching Points
- O_2's backscreen position on the defender should be diagonal.
- The screener's feet should be shoulder-width apart, her arms crossed, and her body balanced.
- O_2 explodes off the screen, rolling to the ball; her hands should be up ready to receive the pass.

Variations
- Add two defenders on O_1 and O_2.
- Pick different spots on the floor to run the screen and roll depending upon the offense run.

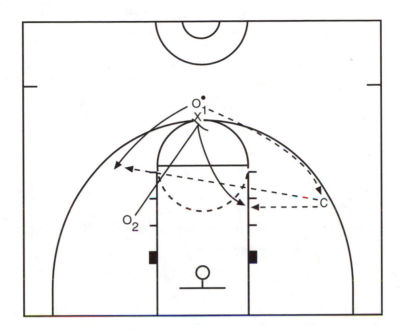

Stagger Drill

Coach Gordy Presnell
School Seattle Pacific University

Purpose
Combination screening drill incorporating the high cut, pick the picker, flair cut, and roll to ball.

Organization
Three lines of players, one coach, and one ball.

Procedure
1. The players are positioned in a two-guard front with a wing.
2. The coach occupies the other wing.
3. A player (O_1) initiates the drill by chest passing to the coach on the right wing.
4. Another player (O_2) and O_1 then move down and to the left to set a double staggered screen on a third player (O_3) who is cutting high (see diagram 1).
5. O_2 then turns and sets a pick-the-picker screen on O_1, who flairs to the weak-side wing.
6. O_2 then rolls to the ball (see diagram 2).
7. A coach may pass to any one of the three cutters.

Coaching Points
- O_3 must jab step baseline to set up her defender. She drives off each screen shoulder to shoulder.
- O_1 flair cuts then quickly backpedals to get in position for a skip pass from the coach.
- O_2 must set the screens and then immediately roll to the strong side looking for the pass.

Variation
Add defenders, initially using one to try to break down the pick-the-picker flair cut. Then add two and three for a full live drill.

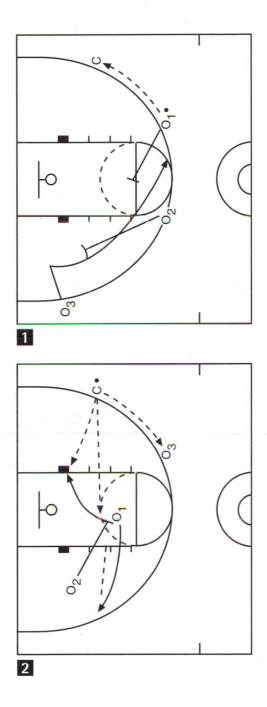

Triangle Downscreen

Coach Gordy Presnell
School Seattle Pacific University

Purpose
To develop proper screening technique and post sealing/pinning while reading the defense.

Organization
Three players with one ball.

Procedure
1. Players set up with a guard (O_1) at the wing with the ball. Another player (O_2) should be at the block and a third (O_3) at the elbow.
2. O_3 walks down and sets a screen on O_2's imaginary defender.
3. O_2 waits for the screen and goes high to the elbow.
4. O_3 posts up.
5. O_1 then passes to O_2, and O_3 reverse seals/pins her imaginary defender.
6. The pass may go inside to O_3 on a pin.

Coaching Points
- The screener should have her arms crossed, her feet shoulder-width apart, her knees slightly bent, and she should be balanced.
- As defense is added, O_1 may dribble baseline to create a better passing angle.

Variation
Add defenders, walk through the drill two times (with live action), and/or rotate.

y

niversity

a screen, using a screen, and
r.

tended at the top of the key,
ne on the block), and one

cond player (O₂).
en rubs shoulders with the

llows her player under the

her teammate about what

the screen (diagram 1). If
2).

creen.

closest to the basket while
th players score.

communication. Players
ut on a cut.

een long enough for O₂ to

hold their positions—but
w the defense to deny or

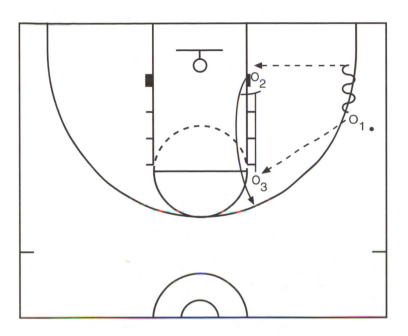

Pin and Spin

Coach Wendy Larry
School Old Dominion University

Purpose
To work on pinning, spinning and sealing the defense after a [been] made on a screen.

Organization
Two passers, each with a ball; one at the top of the key and the oth[er] position. Two offensive players on the blocks with coaches or m[anagers as] defense.

Procedure
1. One player (O$_1$) sets a block-to-block screen for another p[layer]
2. O$_2$ comes off the screen high or low.
3. The defense must switch.
4. The first passer passes to O$_2$, who attempts to score.
5. The second passer passes to O$_1$, who has sealed her defen[se with] the defender pinned on her back. O$_1$ attempts to score.

Coaching Points
- O$_1$ must set a good, low, solid screen, and O$_2$ must set h[er up by] stepping away from the screen and then rubbing off the sho[ulder of the] screener.
- Make sure the screener uses her arms legally to pin and the[n catch the] ball, showing a high target hand.

Variation
Managers can have football blocking pads and bump the cu[tter as they] attempt to score so they get used to finishing with contact.

Off-Ball Scr[een]

Coach Wendy Lar[ry]
School Old Dominion U[niversity]

Purpose
This drill focuses on the fundamentals of setting [and] communicating between the screener and cutte[r.]

Organization
Two passers with one ball each on the lane lines e[ach with] two offensive players (one in the wing and o[ne with a] manager as defense on the block.

Procedure
1. One player (O$_1$) sets a downscreen for a se[cond player]
2. O$_2$ steps to the ball to set up her defense the[n uses the] screener as she cuts off the screen.
3. The defense either fights over the screen or f[ollows the] screen.
4. The screener (O$_1$) must communicate with [O$_2$ whatever] the defense chooses to do.
5. If the defense fights over, O$_2$ should flair of[f, and if] the defense trails, O$_2$ should curl (diagram[)]
6. O$_2$ always steps to the ball after setting her s[creen.]
7. The second passer always passes to the cutte[r, and] the first passer passes to the other player. Bo[th]

Coaching Points
- Emphasize communication—loud, precise[. O$_2$] should call for the ball not only on a screen b[ut]
- Make sure O$_1$ is stationary and holds the scr[een to] come off of it.
- The defense should be *dummy*—that is, just[.] if O$_2$ does not use the screen effectively, all[ow them to] steal the ball.

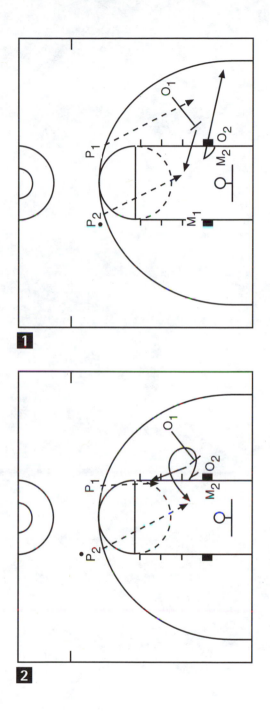

1

2

SHOOTING DRILLS

Great shooters—are they born or made? Whatever your position, there is no doubt that you will have your players' attention when you work on shooting. The feel and sound of a swish is motivation enough for most players to consider how they might improve their shooting fundamentals. And while not all shooters will have the touch of a Carol Blazejowski or the range of a Katie Smith, you can still focus on the work ethic and repetition that all great shooters have in common.

So what will you teach them about shooting that they do not think they already know? Perhaps you are on the side of shooters being born, so you will scan the grade schools and middle schools and seek talented recruits. Or better yet, you will read the following drills and see what new ideas you might incorporate into your skill development plan.

Teaching players how to refine their shots and modify their sometimes counterproductive idiosyncrasies in shooting is a challenge. Assume all shooters (even if they are born with the skills) will benefit from your guidance and development. When you see them put in the extra hours and go the extra mile to gain their rhythm or correct a problem, you will see the results when it is game time!

Depth Shooting

Coach Sonja Hogg
School Baylor University

Purpose
To develop depth perception, movement of the ball, and improved range on shots.

Organization
Two players, one ball, and one basket.

Procedure
1. All shooting is catch and shoot.
2. Start inside the three-point line, then move outside it.
3. One player shoots until she makes 13 shots. The other player rebounds.
4. The players can shoot anywhere inside or outside the three-point line.
5. Use the whole floor, performing an around-the-world movement.
6. For post players, have them work inside then outside the lane.

Coaching Points
- Keep the feet moving at all times so players are ready to go quickly into the shot.
- Don't lose focus when adjusting range.

Variation
Add one or two dribbles off the pass.

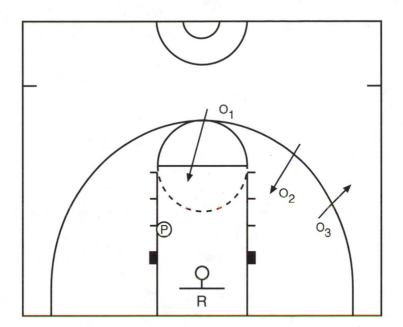

Baylor Shooting Drill

Coach Sonja Hogg
School Baylor University

Purpose
To teach players how to follow their shots.

Organization
One player, one ball, and one basket.

Procedure
1. Make five shots from three spots on the floor. The player picks the spots.
2. Toss and catch, turning on the inside pivot foot.
3. Players can catch and shoot or add moves (e.g., jab and go, fake shot and drive, etc.)
4. Make all five shots from the same spot before moving to the next spot.
5. Follow the shot whether the shot is made or missed. If it's missed, follow and finish until a basket is made.
6. The initial shot only counts toward the five makes.

Coaching Points
- Whether a shot is made or missed, try to follow by not letting the ball hit the floor.
- Go hard at game tempo until all 15 shots are made.
- Put time on the clock to see who can make their 15 first or under a certain time.

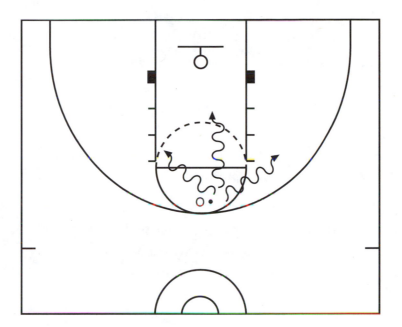

Olympic Shooting

Coach Tara VanDerveer
School Stanford University

Purpose
To practice two varieties of game shots off the move.

Organization
Three players with two balls; shoot for 30 to 45 seconds and keep score. This drill can be competitive among groups.

Procedure
1. Start with one shooter on the perimeter with a ball.
2. One player starts under the basket with a ball.
3. A third player spots up ready to receive the ball from the player under the basket.
4. *Rules:* The shooter gets her own rebound and passes to an open player; after passing, the player spots up for a shot; relocate on every shot.

Coaching Points
- Be within your shooting range but shoot from different spots.
- Be ready to shoot.
- Give a target and make sharp passes.

Variation
The shooter may take three-pointers, pull-ups, or a combination of shots.

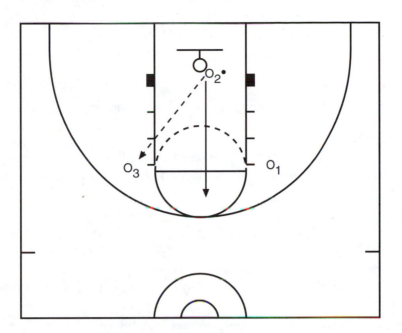

Tick Tock Shooting

Coach Tara VanDerveer
School Stanford University

Purpose
To improve shooting consistency when taking shots at game tempo.

Organization
Everyone gets a partner, and each player has a ball; a coach or manager is a passer. Five minutes are on the clock, and shots will be taken from five perimeter spots.

Procedure
1. If both shooters are taking three-pointers, the goal for shots made from each spot is 10.
2. If both shooters are taking two-pointers, the goal for shots made from each spot is 12.
3. If one shooter is taking three-pointers and the other two-pointers, the goal for shots made from each spot is 11.
4. Each twosome must make their total before moving to the next spot.
5. The goal is for every twosome to finish all five spots before the clock runs out.

Coaching Points
- Take shots in player's range.
- Be ready to shoot; give a target.
- Give sharp passes.

Variation
You may add time for a greater challenge and to increase conditioning.

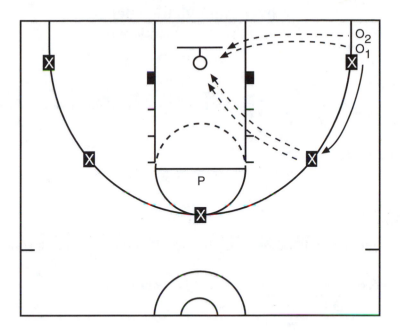

Shooting 100

Coach Tara VanDerveer
School Stanford University

Purpose

To improve shooting consistency and taking shots at game tempo with time pressure.

Organization

Everyone gets a partner; a coach or manager is a passer. Put 12 minutes on the clock. Use five spots and two balls.

Procedure

1. The first player shoots 20 shots from the first spot, and the second player rebounds.
2. The second player shoots 20 from the same spot.
3. They keep alternating shooters until both have taken 20 shots at five spots—100 total per shooter.
4. This should take about 12 minutes.
5. They must shoot at game pace.

Coaching Points

- Take shots in your range.
- Be ready to shoot; give a target.
- Give sharp passes.

Variation

You may add more time for a greater challenge and to increase conditioning.

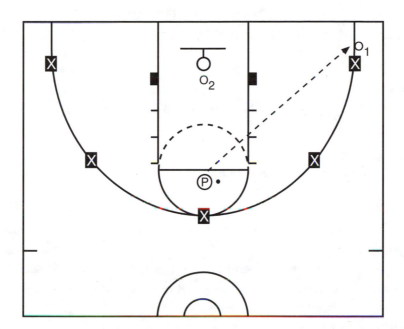

55 Second Drill

Coach Mike Geary
School Northern Michigan University

Purpose

To work on moving into shots, footwork, shooting shots off the catch, and shooting shots under pressure.

Organization

Two players per basket and one ball.

Procedure

1. One player starts with the ball in one of the designated shooting spots (diagrams 1-6).
2. Her partner will rebound and pass to her for the entire 55 seconds.
3. The shooter shoots from one spot and moves to the other spot, receives a pass, and shoots for 55 seconds.
4. At the end of 55 seconds the whistle blows and the partners exchange positions.
5. Five seconds is given to complete the position exchange.
6. The whistle begins the next 55 second set.
7. A manager records the results.

Coaching Points

- Keep moving and time cuts to get to the spot at the same time as the pass.
- When the ball is in the air, get your feet ready to receive the pass.
- The rebounder/passer must work to get the shooter the maximum number of shots.

Variation

The passer passes with her weak hand.

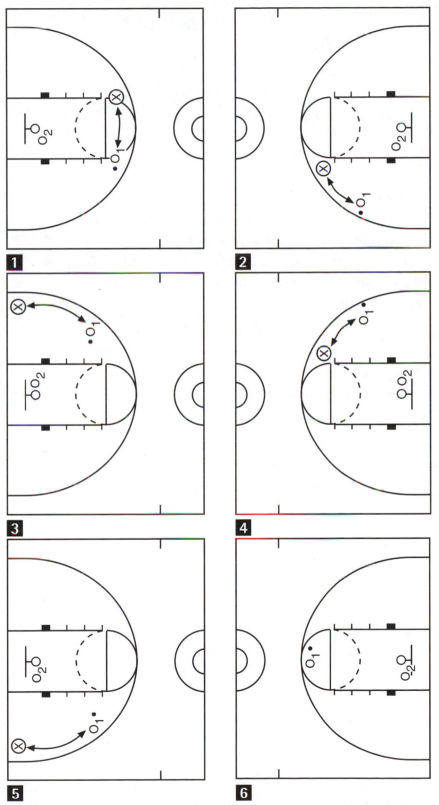

1

2

3

4

5

6

Beat the Clock

Coach Mary Hile-Nepfel
School University of San Francisco

Purpose
To practice shooting under pressure.

Organization
Two players at each basket with one ball.

Procedure
1. Each player works in pairs, and each member of the pair must make six shots before moving to the next spot.
2. Start the drill in the right corner (15- to 17-foot shots).
3. When a pair makes 12 shots, the players all rotate to the next spot (e.g., right wing area).
4. The team is trying to beat the clock (five minutes), making all their shots from the five spots.

Coaching Points
- Emphasize good passes to the shooters.
- Work on a quick release with accuracy.
- It is a team competition. Emphasize teamwork.

Variation
You may increase the number of shots players must make from each spot. Reward the team if they beat the clock.

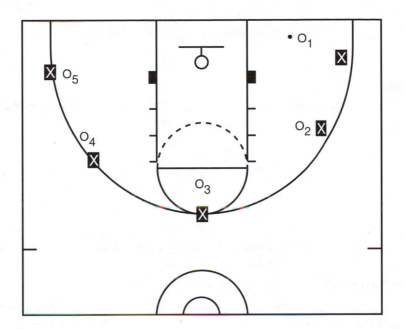

Three-Point Shooting

Coach Mike Geary
School Northern Michigan University

Purpose
To work on three-point shots, passing to teammates on the move, chasing long rebounds, and concentrating under pressure.

Organization
Four lines of three players (as shown in the diagram) with two basketballs in each line.

Procedure
1. The first player in the front of the line shoots a three-point shot from the wing and rebounds her shot.
2. The next player does the same.
3. The third player receives a pass from the first, shoots a three-point shot, and rebounds her shot.
4. The first player now receives a pass from the second.
5. The action continues for two minutes; on the whistle all groups rotate clockwise to the next spot.
6. Total time: eight minutes.

Coaching Points
- Prepare to shoot; have hands and feet ready.
- The passer calls the shooter's name when passing the ball.
- Sprint after the ball and when rotating lines.

Variations
- Stay for one or three minutes at each spot.
- Place four players in each group and use three basketballs.

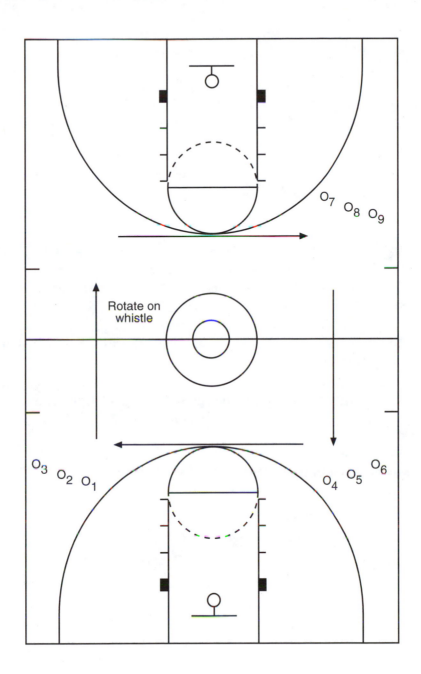

Rotate on whistle

Hilltop Drill

Coach Mary Hile-Nepfel
School University of San Francisco

Purpose

To improve passing and shooting fundamentals.

Organization

Minimum of eight players with three balls; three lines at midcourt and two lines on the baseline with balls.

Procedure

1. Group three players at midcourt with a ball in the middle lane. Start the drill with a chest pass to the left.

2. The player in the right lane sprints to the basket for a layup, receiving a chest pass from the player in the left lane.

3. The two passers on the baseline each throw a pass to the shooters coming in on the left and right wings. Each rebounds her own shot and gets set on the baseline.

4. The player who takes the layup gets her own rebound and outlets to her right. The ball is then passed to the player coming off the left baseline. She then gets the ball back to the middle line.

Coaching Points

- Throw good chest passes to the shooters.
- Do not travel. Practice proper footwork.
- Get the feet set when shooting.

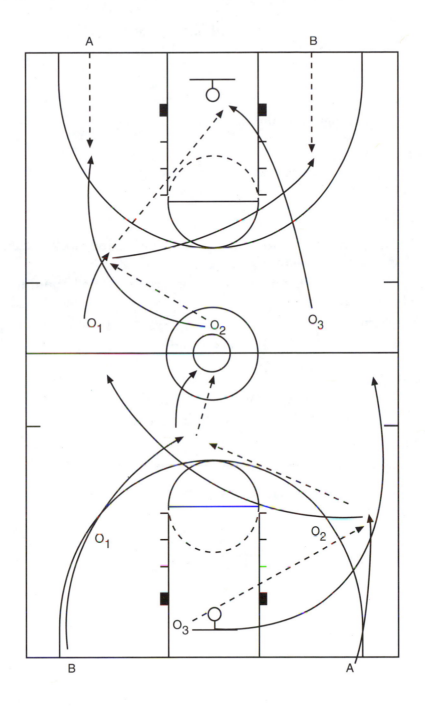

Flash Shooting

Coach Paul Sanderford
School University of Nebraska

Purpose

To improve passing, communication, and shooting.

Organization

One player on the block, one on the opposite wing, and the rest of the players in line at the top of the key with two balls.

Procedure

1. The first pass is made from the top of the key to the block player, who is flashing into the lane.
2. The player catches the pass, squares up, scores, and rebounds to outlet on the wing.
3. She returns the pass back to the top of the key. Everyone follows her pass.
4. Rotate so all players shoot off a post flash.

Coaching Points

- Call for the ball, show a target, and be balanced.
- Be ready to shoot; hustle after shots and rebounds.
- Make strong, crisp outlet passes.

Variation

Move passers to wings and have post players flash up from the blocks to the free throw line for shots.

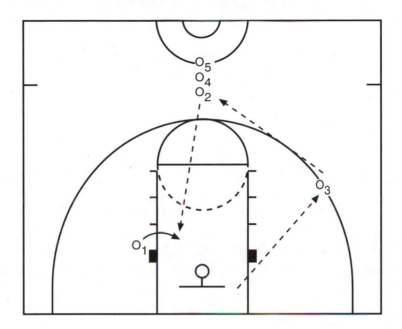

Push and Pull-Up Shooting Drill

Coach Marian Washington
School University of Kansas

Purpose
To work on transition shooting.

Organization
Groups of three start from the baseline; full-court drill. The drill begins with three players passing side-center-side up the floor.

Procedure
1. Pass as the first shooter pulls up from the wing (any spot) for a two-point shot.
2. The shooter gets her own rebound and outlets up the middle of the floor to the opposite wing player.
3. The third player fills the opposite lane (to balance the floor).
4. Shots are taken in this pattern: two-point shot, three-point shot, and one layup.
5. Repeat the pattern of shooting for a designated amount of time (one to two minutes).
6. The team waiting must yell out the score.

Coaching Points
- Good strong passes.
- Focus on sprinting, conditioning, and pushing the ball up the floor.
- Good shooting form; following the shot.

Variations
- Add a clock (one minute) and competitive groups of three. You can assign a goal of 24 points.
- Use short floors and run two teams of three at the same time.
- Reward perfect shooting (no misses) (e.g., no push-ups before getting a drink).

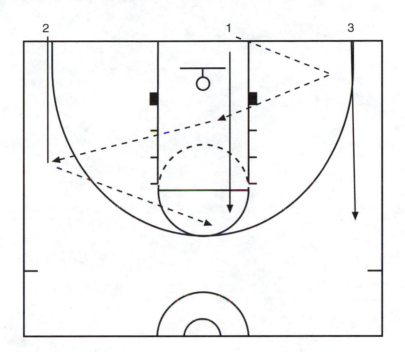

REBOUNDING DRILLS

Finding players who will attack the glass at both ends of the floor and control the boards will make a good coach a winning coach. From the long line of rebounding talent at Louisiana Tech to the agile Lisa Leslie and two-sport phenom Natalie Williams, women's basketball has become a big player's game too! Gone are the days of the tall and slow; the 1990s showcased athletes who could run the floor, rip the boards, and score at the other end.

It's been said that rebounding and defense make the difference in winning programs. With bigger, stronger, and fitter players, rebounding requires a serious gut check for most. There is plenty of contact on the boards and a hearty reward for those who battle well: a quick transition to the other end!

Help your players learn the basics of good offensive rebounding, seeing the angle of the shot, assuming every shot is missed, and pursuing until they have the ball. A little hard work and sweat—not to mention a few bruises—can turn an average player into an invaluable one on the boards.

Coach David Smith
School Bellarman College

Purpose

To teach teams how to rebound off a missed free throw.

Organization

Seven players, a coach or manager, one ball, and one basket.

Procedure

1. Station five individual players around the free throw lane. The coach or manager will shoot the free throws.
2. On the free throw attempt, the defensive players carry out their block-out assignments.
3. After each rebound, the defensive players will rotate clockwise.
4. Once the defensive players have been at each position, switch the offensive and defensive players.

Coaching Points

- Emphasize quickness and making contact as soon as the ball is released or upon hitting the rim, depending upon your rules.
- Emphasize using the proper block-out technique.
- When defensive players know where the ball is going to end up after a missed shot, they release and go get the ball.

Variation

Make this a contest. Award two points for an offensive rebound and one point for a defensive rebound. The first team to 10 points wins.

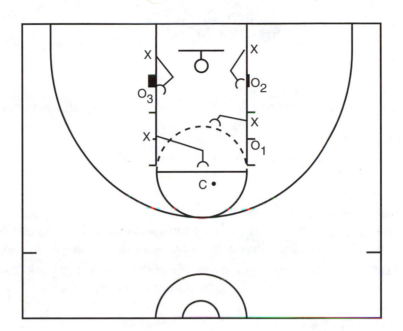

Back Roll Drill

Coach David Smith
School Bellarman College

Purpose
To teach offensive players to roll of a block out to gain an offensive rebound.

Organization
Any number of players, one coach or manager, one ball, and one basket.

Procedure
1. Position a defender in a block-out position facing the basket. Another player is positioned on the rear of the individual blocking out. Station the remainder of the players in a line behind the free throw circle.
2. The coach or manager is off to the side of the lane with a basketball. She or he will toss the ball off the backboard so that it rebounds into the lane.
3. When the ball leaves the coach's hand, the offensive player must roll off the back of the defender (who is not giving any resistance) and go after the ball. The offensive player tries to catch the ball before it hits the floor (see diagram 1).
4. Once the rebound has been secured, the offensive player will keep the ball high, step to the basket, and put the ball in the basket. If she is more than one step from the basket, she should take a dribble.
5. The offensive player then becomes the defender and the defender goes to the end of the line.

Coaching Points
- Emphasize that the offensive player does a 360-degree roll off the defender.
- Emphasize that the offensive player should keep her hands up in front of her as she rolls since the ball will often hit her hands before she visually finds the ball.
- The coach should move to each side of the lane so players will roll each direction. Some can roll one way but struggle going the other.

Variation
In teaching offensive players to roll, you can adjust their drill by having a single player at the free throw line, letting that player throw the ball off the board, do a 360-degree roll, catch the ball, and put it back in the basket.

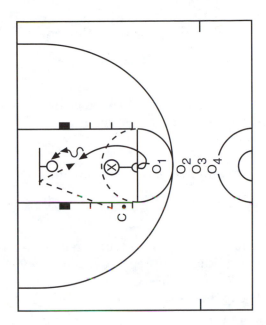

Five-on-Two Block-Out Drill

Coach David Smith
School Bellarman College

Purpose

To teach players to find someone to block out, go to that player and make contact, find the ball, release, and go get the ball.

Organization

Seven players, any combination of two coaches and/or managers, one ball, and one basket.

Procedure

1. Put five individual players around the three-point circle. Two defenders will be in the middle of the free throw lane. They will be facing away from the basket. A coach will be under the basket, and another coach or manager will be on the perimeter with a basketball.

2. The coach under the basket will designate two players on the perimeter (by pointing at them).

3. When the coach has designated the offensive players, the coach or manager shoots the ball. The two designated offensive players go for the rebound, and the defense must locate the designated offensive players, move to them, and block them out. The defender holds her block out until she locates the ball, then releases and goes to get the rebound (see diagram 1).

4. Once the rebound has been secured either by the defense or offense, the ball is returned to the coach on the perimeter. The offensive players go back to their original positions, the defense returns to the middle of the lane, and the drill is repeated with the same or a different combination of offensive players being designated.

Coaching Points

- Emphasize that the initial defensive contact with the offensive players must be outside the lane.
- Emphasize proper block-out technique.
- When the defense knows where the ball is going to end up after a missed shot, they must release and go get the ball.
- The defense must communicate who they are going to block out so that both don't go to the same offensive player.
- When the coach is satisfied with the efforts of the defense, they will change positions with two of the offensive players on the perimeter.

Variations

If you are working with young players and just beginning to teach blocking out or you don't have someone to shoot the ball, you can make these adjustments to the drill:

- Have only one defender in the middle (diagram 2).
- Place a ball on the floor behind the defense.
- Designate only one offensive player to go for the ball and be blocked out.
- After designating the offensive player, the coach can blow his or her whistle for the drill to begin.
- Have defense hold the block out until the coach blows their whistle (three to five seconds after the initial contact).
- The number of players on the perimeter can be reduced to three or four.

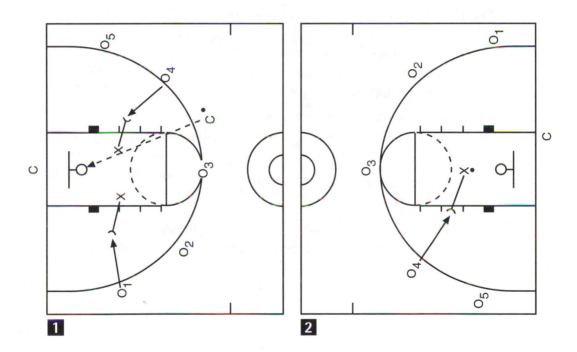

Sixer's Rebounding Drill

Coach Debbie Ryan
School University of Virginia

Purpose

To rebound out of player-to-player situations (i.e., helping positioning on the ball and denying the next pass positions).

Organization

Five offensive players on the baseline, five defensive players at half-court, and two coaches in the far corners of the court near the baseline.

Procedure

1. The five offensive players weave (passing the ball) to half-court (diagram 1).

2. The five defensive players await their turn at the half-court line.

3. When the offensive players get to half-court, the ball is passed long to a coach in either corner (diagram 2).

4. The defense must react to where the ball is relative to the player they've just picked up.

5. The coach shoots immediately, and the defense must box out a rebound ball to either coach in the corner (diagram 3).

Coaching Points

- As the five-person weave occurs, the defense works on communicating and matching up.
- As the ball is passed, the defense must get into proper positions.
- The defense should maintain a box out and throw good strong outlet passes.

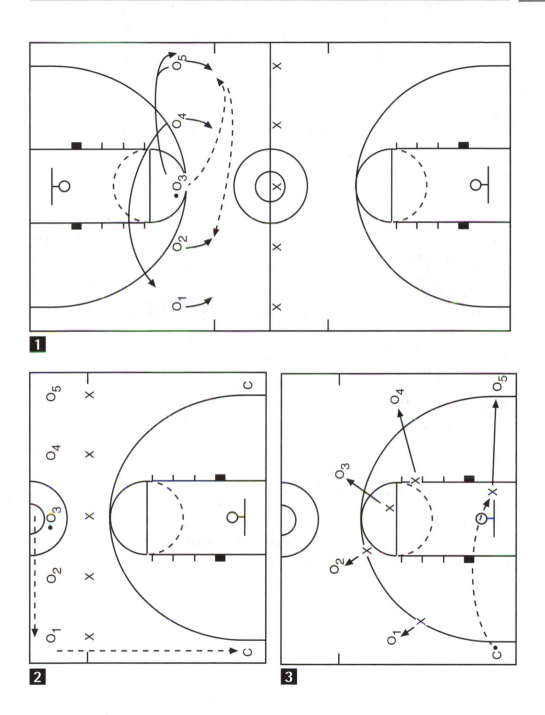

1

2

3

Hit and Rebound

Coach Patrick Knapp
School Georgetown University

Purpose
To work on team reaction and reading angles on rebounds.

Organization
Four or more players, one ball, two lines, and one coach.

Procedure
1. Line up pairs of players at either elbow—two offensive and two defensive.
2. The coach should have the ball in the key area. The defense is in a defensive stance, and the offense is in a ready position.
3. The coach yells "go," and the defense hits the deck (does a quick push-up).
4. The coach shoots the ball as the defense stands up. The defense must adjust, use box-out footwork, make contact, see the rim, and get the ball.

Coaching Points
- Timing of the toss or shot is key.
- Emphasize that players should react and hustle.
- No holding—use proper box-out footwork.
- The offense becomes the defense, and the defense goes off.

Variation
Don't let the defense off until they get one or more rebounds. The offense must attack the basket with fakes and spins.

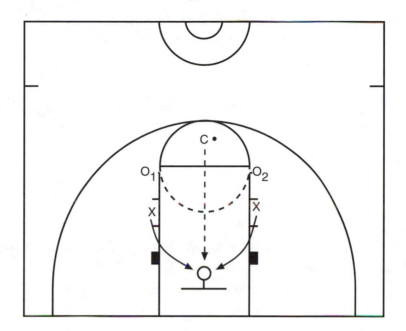

Two-Ball Rebounding Drill

Coach Patrick Knapp
School Georgetown University

Purpose
To teach players to use extra effort when offensive rebounding and to box out, rebound, and outlet the ball.

Organization
Three offensive players and three defensive players, two coaches or managers, and two balls.

Procedure
1. The drill involves three-on-three competition between the offense and defense.
2. Start the drill with the coach or manager shooting the ball.
3. If the defense gains control, outlet to the coach or manager.
4. If the offense gains control, they should try to score.
5. As soon as the first ball is controlled, the coach or manager shoots a second ball.
6. Both groups rebound both shots. Continue the drill until the offense rebounds and scores.

Coaching Points
- The defense should always make contact and move to the ball.
- The offense should go after the rebounds with reckless abandon. The offense stops, cuts, and spins to get into position.

Variation
The coach can have players screen, move, and cut in three-on-three motion concepts in order to change the defense's position.

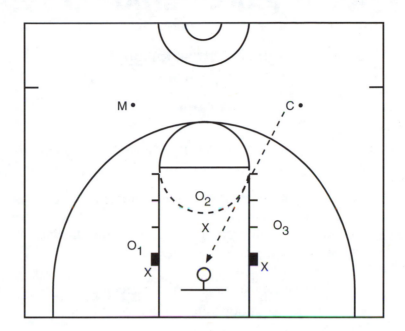

Two-on-Two Weak-Side Rebounding

Coach Patrick Knapp
School Georgetown University

Purpose
To work on defending and boxing out against a screen and cut offense.

Organization
Two offensive players (one at the baseline and one at the wing), two defensive players (one at the baseline and one at the wing), two coaches or managers at the top of the circle on opposite sides, and one ball.

Procedure
1. Line up in a two-on-two weak-side downscreen position.
2. The coach or manager is opposite the guard and the wing.
3. The ball starts in the offensive guard's hands.
4. Upon passing to the coach, the players should go into a downscreen movement (see diagram 1).
5. Proper offensive and defensive screening rules apply.
6. The coach can shoot the ball or pass to the manager, who shoots from the wing or corner (diagram 2).

Coaching Points
- The defense should talk, see the ball, and play the help side.
- The defense should make contact, force the offense one way, and pivot the other.
- The offense should cut and spin to the hoop and rebound with reckless abandon.

Variations
Play live. If the coach or manager sees an open player, he or she should pass it. Here are some other variations:
- Three possessions then switch, or the defense can stay on until they stop or rebound.
- Make the defense sprint or do a push-up for every offensive rebound.
- Teach offensive rebounding steps, cuts, and spins.

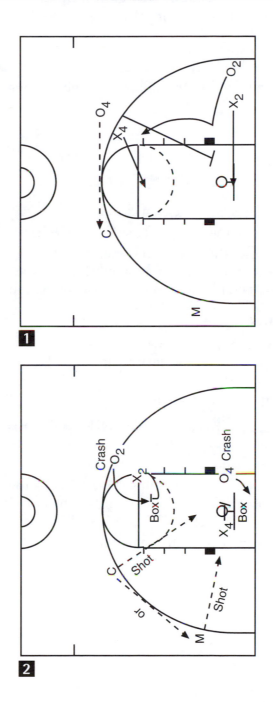

Figure-Eight Rebounding

Coach Patrick Knapp
School Georgetown University

Purpose
To teach players ball control while tipping and rebounding as a conditioning drill.

Organization
Three players at a basket with one ball.

Procedure
1. Place three players and a ball at each basket.
2. The ball starts on the two-player side of the rim.
3. One player tosses the ball on an angle above the basket and across the board to create a rebound for another player. As this is done, the first player moves behind the second. (*Tip:* Rebound and go behind.)

Coaching Points
- Younger players may catch it with two hands and come down, chin the ball, and go back up. Older players can tip with one or two hands and keep the ball moving.
- When tipping, keep the ball high.
- Rebound the ball with two hands at the peak of the jump.
- Emphasize balance and control.
- Use proper two-hand and two-foot techniques
- Designate a certain number of tips (15, 20, 25 in a row) or tipping for a certain amount of time (30, 45, 60 seconds). The last player finishes with a basket.
- Attack the ball and constantly be moving.

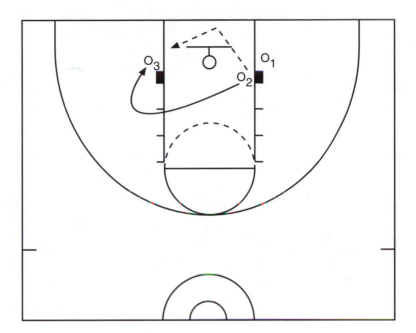

Three-Line Rebounding

Coach Theresa Grentz
School University of Illinois

Purpose
To teach multiple efforts in securing rebounds.

Organization
Three lines of players at the three-point circle. One line should be at each wing and one line at the top of the key. The first person in each line is the defender; the second person is the offensive player. The coach has the ball and begins anywhere on the court she or he desires.

Procedure
1. The defense begins the drill by slapping the floor from a defensive stance and yelling "defense."
2. The coach begins the drill by shooting and intentionally missing a shot.
3. The offensive players attempt to rebound, and the defensive players box out first and then rebound.
4. If the offense rebounds, the offensive player puts the ball back up immediately from the spot of the rebound.
5. If the defense rebounds, the defender outlets the basketball to the person in the closest wing position, and that person dribbles the full length of the court and scores the layup.
6. While the ball is in transition to the other end, the defense steps off and the offense becomes the defense; a new offense steps up.
7. The coach is ready for another missed shot.
8. The drill is continuous, and changing of defense and offense should occur quickly.

Coaching Points
- This drill teaches the offense to make multiple attempts to gain a rebound, and it teaches the defense to hold their box-out position until their team can secure the rebound.
- Emphasize intensity and focus by players to complete the task. The transition is important and needs to be emphasized.

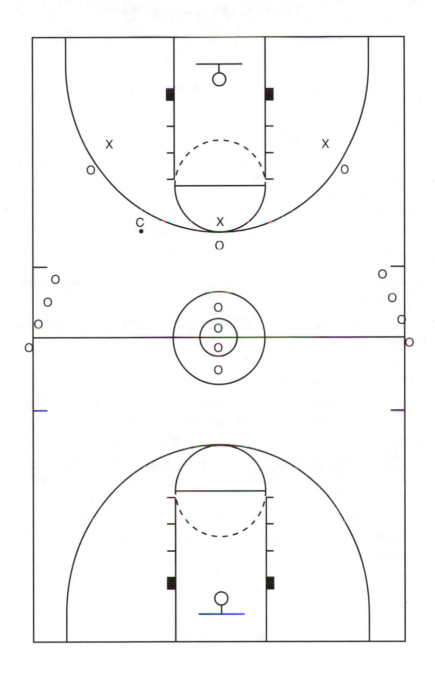

Three-on-Three, Three-on-Four

Coach Theresa Grentz
School University of Illinois

Purpose
To work on shell defense positioning, boxing out and rebounding, transition, execution, and transition defense.

Organization
Four defensive players (team A), three offensive players (team B), one ball, and one coach.

Procedure
1. The coach has the ball.
2. Team B passes and moves, keeping the floor spread and forcing team A to play defense.
3. Only the coach can shoot the ball (you can decide if the offense can score another way, such as only off a layup).
4. Once the shot is taken, team A boxes out and rebounds the ball (if the shot is made, team A takes the ball out of bounds).
5. Team A outlets the ball and transitions down to the other end with team B now on defense (four-on-three situation; see diagram 1).
6. Team A is working on scoring when they have a numerical advantage (in diagram 2).
7. On the shot, team B is now boxing out and rebounding. Outlet the ball and transition back to the original end of the court. Team A is again on defense (see diagram 3).
8. Team B is working on scoring when they have a numerical disadvantage (see diagram 4).
9. Upon scoring, stop play and reset the drill.
10. You can bring on a new team or switch offense to defense.

Coaching Points
- Emphasize boxing out and rebounding.
- Transition offense with a numerical advantage.
- Transition defense with a numerical disadvantage

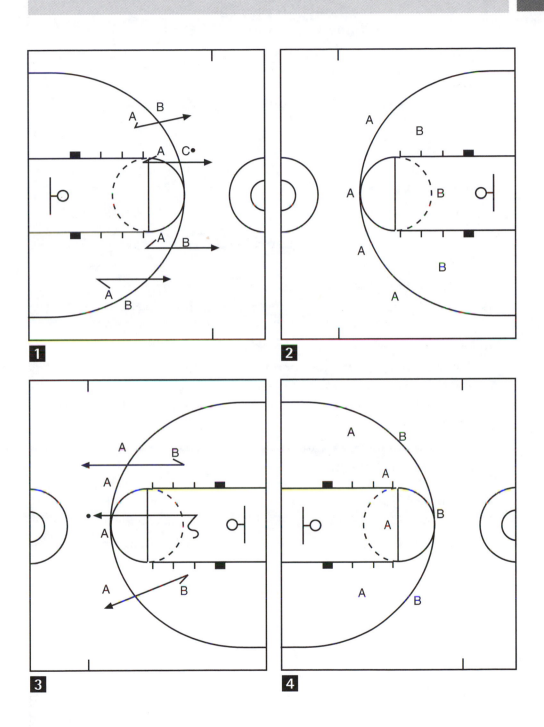

Competitive Rebounding

Coach Nancy Fahey
School Washington University

Purpose
To help reinforce rebounding position in a two-on-two competitive situation.

Organization
Two lines on either side of the lane; defenders will be under the basket; the offense will be in two lines at the elbows.

Procedure
1. Two-on-two (team A versus team B) and no dribbling.
2. Team A passes the ball to team B. Team B shoots off the pass.
3. Team A follows the pass, defends the shot, and boxes out.
4. Even if the shot is made, play it as a missed shot and continue to battle for the rebound.
5. Team B crashes the offensive boards.
6. The team that gets the rebound goes to the group at the elbows. The other team goes under the basket.
7. The goal is to end up at the elbows. The group under the basket receives some type of consequence (e.g., sprints, push-ups).
8. The drill continues with another pair of teams.
9. The duration of the drill is two minutes.

Coaching Points
- Watch for excessive fouling.
- Keep the drill moving and switch players so they go against different competitors from time to time.

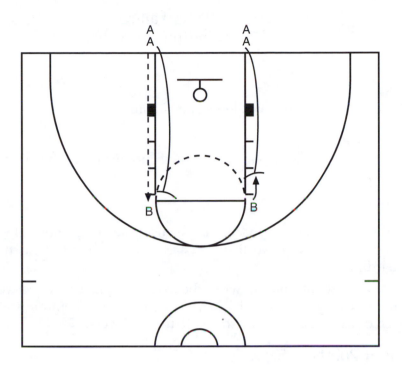

Circle Box Out

Coach Nancy Fahey
School Washington University

Purpose
To help simulate zone rebounding responsibilities.

Organization
Three stationary offensive players and three moving defensive players (see the diagram).

Procedure
1. On a signal from the coach, the defense rotates positions clockwise. Every time they move they must call out by name who they are guarding.
2. The coach shoots the ball when the defensive players are between the offensive players and the basket. The defense must communicate with each other and box out all three offensive players.

Coaching Points
- You should not allow the defense to doubleteam offensive players.
- The offense should crash the boards.
- All defensive players should move while in their defensive stance.

Variation
As the defensive players are circling clockwise, the coach will yell "switch." The defense then changes directions and rotates counterclockwise. Again, the coach shoots the ball when the defense is between the offensive players and the basket.

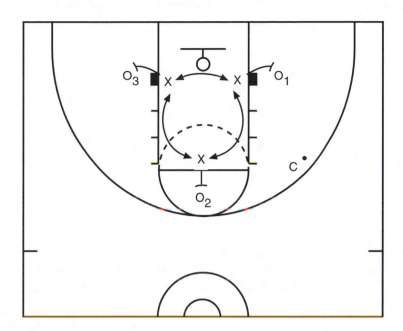

Three-Player Weave— Weak-Side Box Out

Coach Nancy Fahey
School Washington University

Purpose
To reinforce backside rebounding responsibilities (can be used as a warm-up).

Organization
Three lines at half-court.

Procedure
1. O_1 passes to O_2, who dribbles hard to the extended free throw line as O_1 circles behind her. O_3 sprints to the middle of the lane in a defensive position (see diagram 1).
2. O_2 passes back to O_1, who is now at the wing, then reverses to the opposite wing area (see diagram 2).
3. O_1 executes a front crossover dribble to the baseline and pulls up for a jumper (diagram 2).
4. O_3 must turn and find O_2 on the backside and box her out.
5. The drill repeats with three different players.

Coaching Points
- The defensive player's first look on the shot is to box out O_2. She must step toward O_2, not toward the basket.
- Most rebounds come off the opposite side of the basket from the shot; therefore it is important that the weak-side rebounder has a good angle to rebound the basketball.

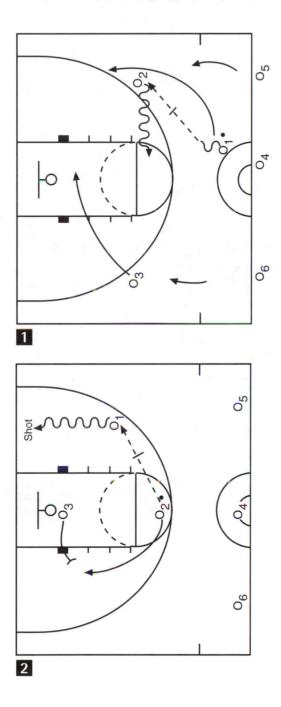

1

2

Box Out and Go

Coach Jody Conradt
School University of Texas

Purpose
To improve boxing out and making the outlet pass to start an offensive transition.

Organization
The coach or manager is the shooter at the free throw line. An offensive and a defensive player match up on either side of the lane about midway down. Players should form outlet lines on either side of the floor.

Procedure
1. When the shot goes up, each defender must box out her player and secure the rebound (diagram 1).
2. The ball should be outletted to the nearest side outlet player.
3. The two outlet players take the ball two-on-one (versus the rebounder) to the other end of the floor and convert (diagram 2).

Coaching Points
- The offense rotates to become the defense.
- The next two players in each outlet line become offensive players.

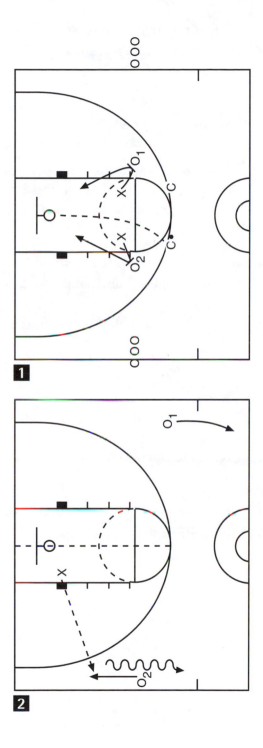

Rebound Outlet

Coach Trina Patterson
School College of William and Mary

Purpose
To develop good ball handling, passing, and rebounding skills.

Organization
Half the team should go to the rebound line under the basket and should have a ball; a partner for each player should be at the three-point line as an outlet.

Procedure
1. The rebounder tosses the ball off the backboard and retrieves it.
2. The outlet player calls "outlet" and steps to receive a pass then squares up to face up the floor.
3. The outlet player dribbles the ball to the middle of the floor and slightly to the left.
4. The rebounder passes to the outlet player and fills the right lane, calling "right."
5. The outlet player delivers a pass to the rebounder, who is cutting hard for a layup.
6. The passer rebounds; the shooter becomes the outlet player on the return trip to the opposite end of the court.

Coaching Points
- Allow every player the opportunity to work on her ballhandling skills.
- Emphasize that ball handlers should push the ball hard up the floor.

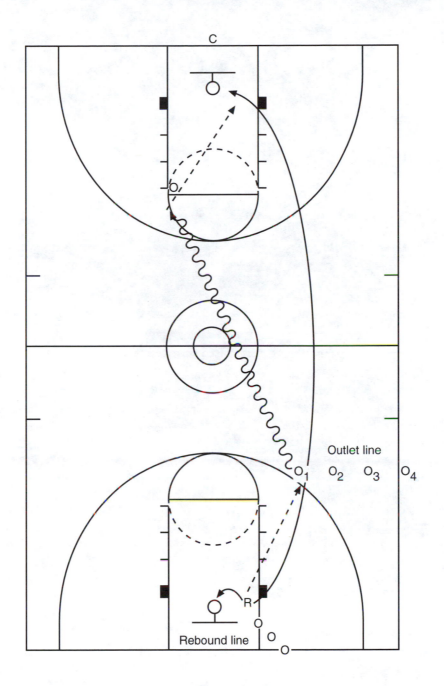

C

Outlet line

O_1 O_2 O_3 O_4

R

Rebound line

7

TRANSITION DRILLS

Transition basketball comes in many packages. The speed and savvy of Old Dominion, the disciplined precision of Tennessee, and the wide-open attack of Stanford all aim to accomplish the same goal: to score at the other end when they have an advantage.

Without a doubt, transition offense is the closest thing to playground ball; however, skills, discipline, and creativity all must blend into the team philosophy. Thus the many different looks of the transition game. Some teams attack fast and furiously; others alternate their pace to catch their defenders off guard. Some shoot quickly and from long range, while others only attempt layups. Whatever your team's style, putting your plan into action involves a lot of preliminary steps. Who will handle the ball? Will the ball come up the sideline or the middle? Will it be dribbled or passed? Who is your primary attacker off a drive or a pull up? Answer these questions first, then read on into the following drills and put your plan into action!

Transition Post Up

Coach Sonja Hogg
School Baylor University

Purpose

To help teach post players how to post up in transition.

Organization

Two players—one on offense and one on defense, one ball, one blocking dummy, and one passer/coach.

Procedure

1. The offense starts on the block, rebounds the ball off the glass, and outlets to the coach on the wing.
2. The offense sprints to the free throw line then sprints back to the block to post up against the defense (diagram 1).
3. The defense waits *above* the block with the blocking dummy.
4. The offense must create contact with the defense and post up to receive a pass from the wing.
5. The offense will then drop step to the middle and score (diagram 2).
6. The offense takes the ball out of the basket, rebounds again, and sprints to half-court and back to the block. Repeat this to the opposite free throw line and back to complete the drill.

Coaching Points

- The offense should pivot to the outside to make an outlet pass.
- The offense may sprint to the free throw line, to half-court, and then to the opposite free throw line before coming back to post up (for conditioning).
- The offense should create contact then post up. Do not let the offense back into the defense.

Variations

- Coaches/managers can be used for passing and/or defense.
- Once this technique is learned, the offense and defense can go live without the blocking dummy to simulate a game situation.

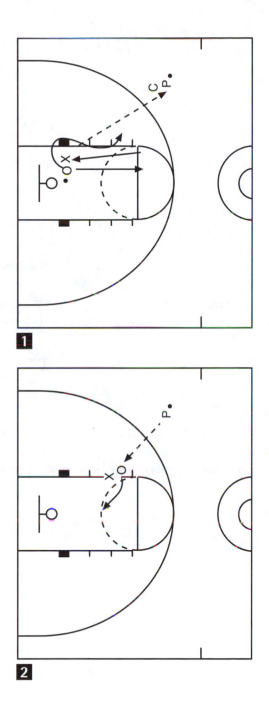

Catch Up

Coach Muffet McGraw
School University of Notre Dame

Purpose
To work on offense's transition to defense, learning how to work in a three-on-two situation defensively.

Organization
Three defenders line up along the free throw line, and three offensive players line up on the baseline using one ball.

Procedure
1. The coach throws the ball to any of the three offensive players on the baseline.
2. Whoever has lined up across from the offensive player is her defender; this player runs to touch the baseline while the offense takes off three-on-two.
3. The third defender sprints to catch up and then play becomes three-on-three.

Coaching Points
- The defense should communicate and form a tandem until the third defender arrives.
- Usually, the last defender down guards whoever is at the top of the key.

Variation
Play it live and come back down the court three-on-three using full-court pressure.

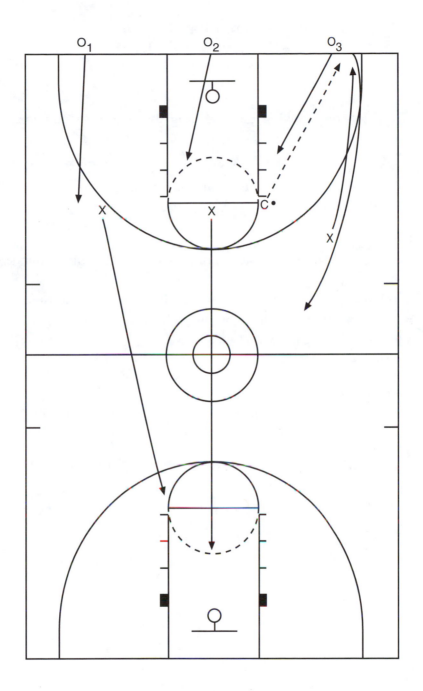

Break on Numbers

Coach Muffet McGraw
School University of Notre Dame

Purpose

After a quick score, looking up, throwing the ball ahead, making good decisions, and finding the open player.

Organization

Nine to 10 players: five on offense at one end of the court (in the lane); everyone else is at half-court out of bounds; one ball is used.

Procedure

1. The coach misses a shot, and the offense rebounds, outlets, and fills the lane.
2. Another coach is at half-court and sends out one to four defenders.
3. The offense must find the open player and try to score quickly.
4. When the play is over, the offense stays in the lane and the defense returns to half-court; the coach shoots, and the drill is repeated.

Coaching Points

- Everyone rebounds; you may run a pattern, break, or just fill the lanes.
- Turn to the outside for an outlet pass; the point guard calls for the ball.
- Run hard and run wide on the wings.

Variation

Send more defenders (up to five) to catch up to the ball.

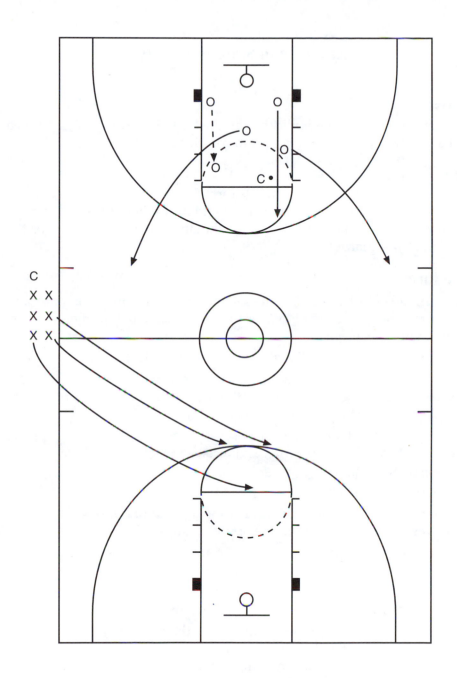

Post Up Out Front

Coach Rene Portland
School Penn State University

Purpose

To improve a post player's ability to run the floor while also working on a guard's ability to pass the ball ahead in transition.

Organization

Three players use one ball. The guards form two lines, one at the extended foul line (out of bounds) in the back court and the other at the hash mark in the front court. Post players form a line on the elbow in the back court (on the same side as the guards).

Procedure

1. The first post player in line tosses the ball off of the backboard and secures the rebound. The player then outlets the ball to the guard on their end of the court.

2. The guard passes the ball to the second guard at the far end of the court.

3. After outletting the ball, the post player sprints the floor looking for a fast-break layup. Meanwhile, the guard dribbles into position to make a good post entry pass (diagram 1).

4. The guard can either pass to the post player on the fly, or the post player can establish post-up position and receive the pass from the guard.

5. On the shot, the guard comes to the middle of the lane to establish rebounding position.

6. After scoring, the post player takes the ball out of bounds. The guard moves to the outlet spot on the opposite side of the floor.

7. The post player inbounds the ball to the guard and sprints the floor (diagram 2).

8. The guard takes a few dribbles then passes ahead to the post player. The post player finishes the play with an uncontested layup.

9. The post player then moves to the end of the post line with a new post player initiating the drill. The guard goes to the end of the back court line, with the other guard moving to the front court line.

Coaching Points

- The post player should be conscious of where the ball is at all times.
- The guard, on the return trip down the floor, should pass to the post player just after the post player has crossed half-court.

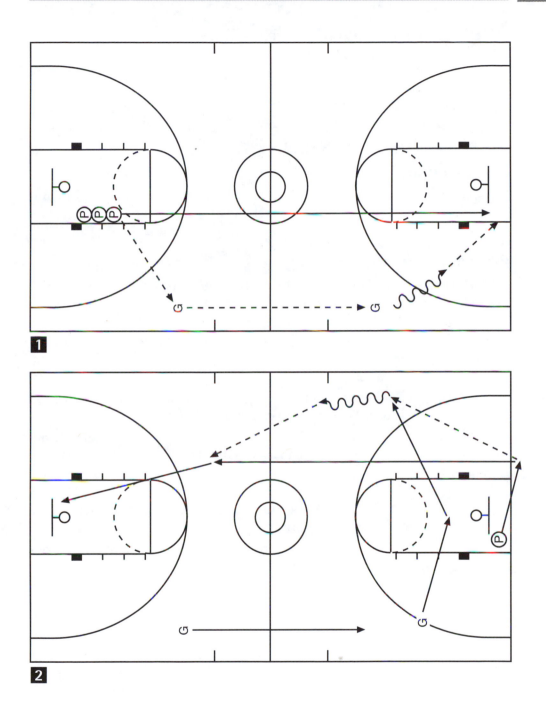

1

2

Five-Lane Recognition Drill

Coach Barbara Stevens
School Bentley College

Purpose

To teach recognition of filling lanes on a fast break. This drill stresses communication and is a great conditioner.

Organization

Five players: a rebounder, an outlet, a middle, a left wing, and a right wing with one ball. All players are positioned below the top of the extended three-point circle.

Procedure

1. The ball is tossed off the backboard by the rebounder to start the drill. The remaining players break to the outlet, middle, right wing, and left wing.
2. The rebounder throws the ball to the outlet, who then passes to the middle, then to the left wing, and finally to the right wing for the layup (diagram 1).
3. All players must sprint the floor, cross midcourt, and on the return must change positions. They need to call out their positions!
4. The ball should not be dribbled. It must not touch the floor until the final pass, which can be a bounce pass. It will take four passes to score.

Coaching Points

- Players must verbalize their positions and must learn to see what lanes are filled; they must then sprint to the open lane!
- Players must call out their positions to alert the passer of the next pass (e.g., "outlet," "middle," "left," "right," or "rebound").

Variation

This drill can be run up and back two times, or to add more of a conditioning aspect it can be run several more times. (See diagram 2.)

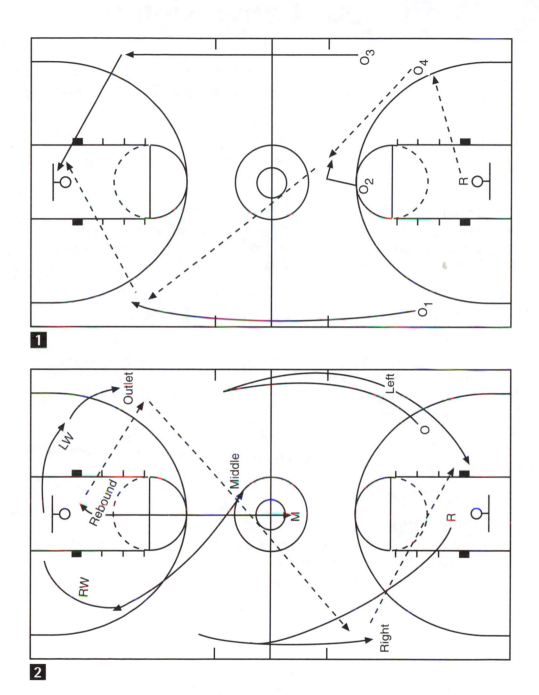

74 Three-on-Two, Two-on-One Continuous Conversion Drill

Coach Barbara Stevens
School Bentley College

Purpose
To teach offensive and defensive decision making in numerical advantage and disadvantage situations.

Organization
Players begin the drill on the endline with the ball in the middle. Two tandem defenders start in the center circle. The rest of the team is split into two outlet lines at one end of the court.

Procedure
1. The three offensive players attack the two defenders.
2. If the offense scores or the defense gets possession, the two defenders come back on offense against the last player to touch the ball on offense (two-on-one). (See diagram 1.)
3. The two remaining (formerly) offensive players go to the center court circle to become the next tandem defenders (see diagram 2).
4. Only allow one shot in the two-on-one segment. Whether it's made or missed, any one of the three players may outlet the ball to one of the outlet lines and fill a lane in the next group of three to attack the waiting tandem defense.

Coaching Points
- Limit the number of passes the offense makes to score. The more passes made, the more time the defenders have to recover.
- Pass the ball ahead to shift the defense.
- Defenders need to talk, shift quickly, and not force the offense into several passes.

Variation
Run this drill for a designated amount of time. It is competitive and can reward the player who hustles to stay in the drill!

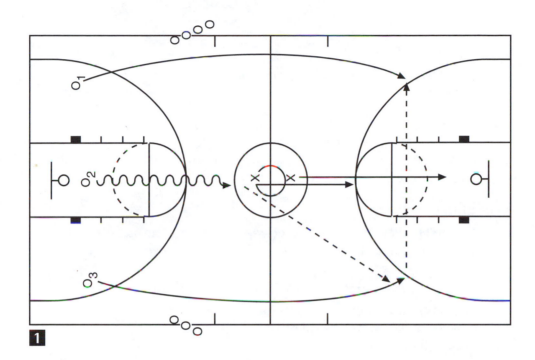

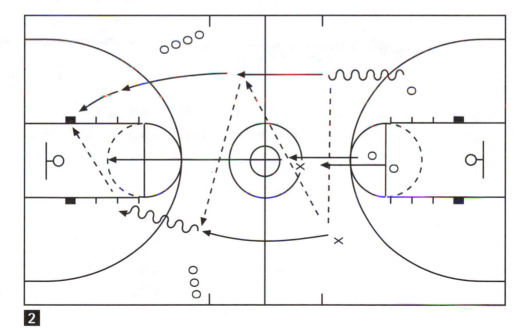

Celtics Fast-Break Drill

Coach Barbara Stevens
School Bentley College

Purpose
To work on the execution of full-court layups and the baseball outlet pass. A good conditioner!

Organization
Players are split into two groups, one group under the basket and the other in an outlet line on the sideline approximately along the extended free throw line. Two or three balls are needed.

Procedure
1. The first player under the basket steps out, tosses the ball off the board, and throws an outlet pass to the first player in the outlet line.
2. The outlet player speed dribbles down the court and takes a layup. The rebounder sprints to follow the shot and puts back any misses.
3. The rebounder then takes a made shot out of bounds and throws a baseball pass to the first player, who is sprinting down the sideline. This player speed dribbles and takes the layup.
4. The next rebounder waiting takes the ball out of the net, outlets to the next player in the outlet line, and they repeat the drill.
5. This is a continuous drill; the new group can begin when the first layup is taken at the opposite end of the floor.

Coaching Points
- Call for an outlet pass. Execute a good overhead outlet pass.
- Throw the baseball pass over the receiver's inside shoulder.

Variations
- Run this drill on both sides of the floor.
- Run it for a designated amount of time or until a certain number of layups is reached.
- You can keep players in the same lines or have them change lines.
- The shooter can pull up for a jumper or a three-pointer.

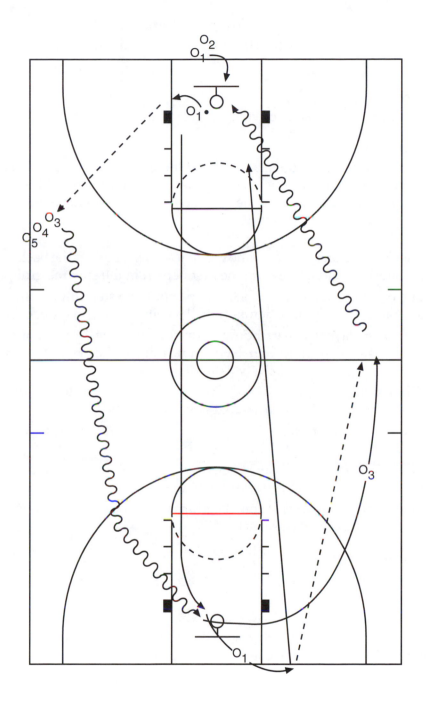

Air It Out

Coach Theresa Grentz
School University of Illinois

Purpose
To teach transition passing, catching, and shooting; great for conditioning.

Organization
Divide the team into two equal groups. One group should be under the basket outside the free throw lane, and the second group should be out of bounds in the wing area along the sideline. Two balls to start the drill.

Procedure
1. The first person in the baseline group tosses the ball off the backboard, rebounds it, and passes it to the first person in the sideline group.
2. The first person in the sideline group should be stepping on the court to assume the wing position as the ball is being tossed off the backboard.
3. The wing player receives the outlet, dribbles the length of the court, and executes a layup. The original rebounder follows the play, rebounds the made layup, and takes the ball out of bounds.
4. The shooter (O_4), after having made the layup, breaks to the opposite wing and runs long and wide down the sideline.
5. The shooter receives the pass from O_1 and executes a layup, with the passer (O_1) following the play to rebound the shot.
6. The ball is passed to the next person in the baseline group and the two players involved in the drill switch lines.
7. The next pair of players begin their turn when the first layup is made at the opposite end of the court.

Coaching Points
- For players to throw a long pass with accuracy, proper technique for the release of the pass and proper control of the spin of the ball should be emphasized.
- To use the drill for conditioning, it should be performed for a minimum of two minutes on each side of the basket.

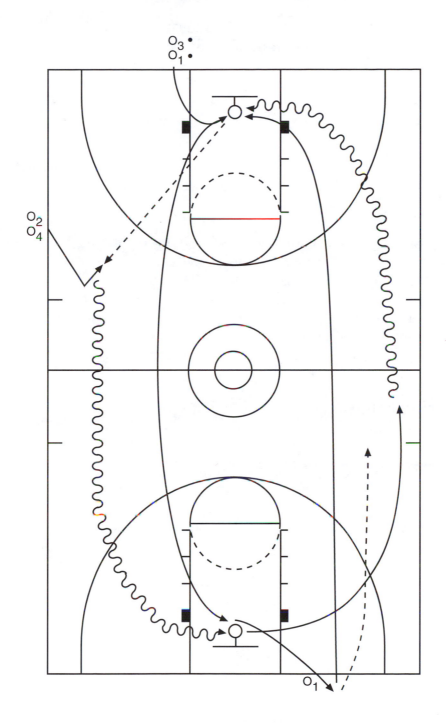

Weave Shooting

Coach Bob Lindsay
School Kent State

Purpose
To develop full-speed passing and shooting in transition.

Organization
Three lines of players on both baselines and four balls, one on the baseline where the drill starts and three on the opposite baseline.

Procedure
1. Three players weave from one baseline to the other.
2. The first shooter—the player who has the ball at the end of the weave—makes a layup, rebounds, and steps off the court.
3. The second and third players receive diagonal skip passes from baseline passers for 15-foot shots or three-pointers, rebound, and step off the court (diagram 1).
4. The next group starts a weave from the baseline and repeats the drill; the middle player starts the group (diagram 2).

Coaching Points
- No turnovers; penalty for missed shots.
- Have shooting percentage goals and a time limit.
- Run at full speed, stay wide, and communicate.

Variation
Shoot different shots.

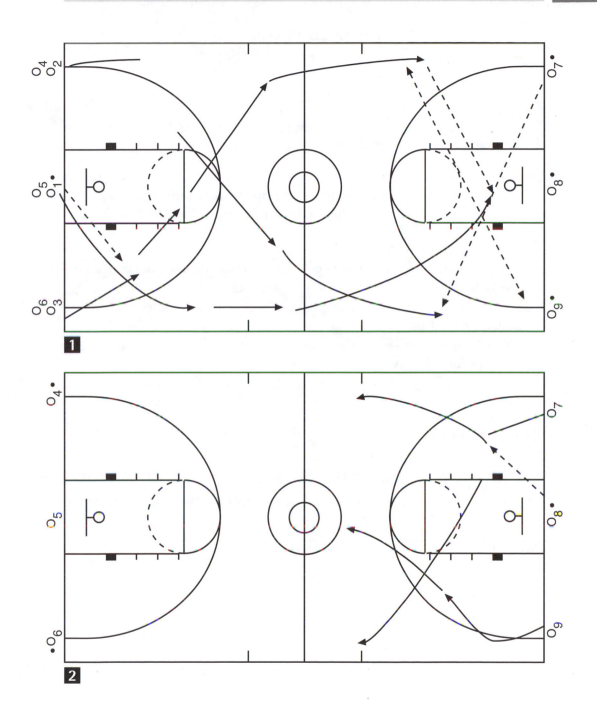

1

2

Big Player, Little Player Drill

Coach Marian Washington
School University of Kansas

Purpose
To enhance the open-court (two-on-one) breakaway transition game and to develop great passing. Great conditioning drill.

Organization
Two lines of players on the baseline; one line of forwards and posts (big players) and the other line of guards (little players); use three balls.

Procedure
1. Forward or post (big player) gets the rebound off the backboard and outlets to the guard (little player); use three balls.
2. The big player sprints out at the free throw line extended to the sideline and fills the lane.
3. The guard dribbles up the floor and makes a good pass to the big player for a layup.
4. The next pair go from the opposite baseline as the first group of two complete the shot.

Coaching Points
- Strong, crisp, and accurate passes.
- Competitive, team effort. Set a goal and make it!
- The coach calls the shot (pull up, jump shots off one dribble, or reverse layup only).

Variation
Competitive drill. *Example:* Two minutes for 30 baskets with two or fewer time outs.

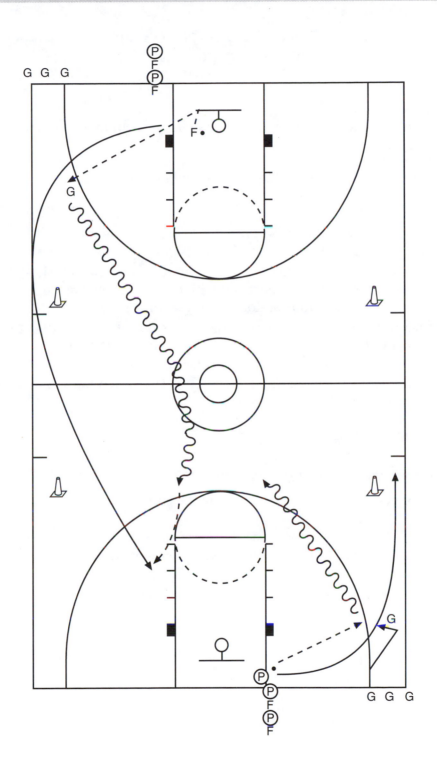

Coach Kathy Delaney-Smith
School Harvard University

Purpose
To teach transition principles, teamwork, and poise under pressure.

Organization
Four players on each team, three teams, and one ball.

Procedure
1. The first team (A) starts at half-court with the ball and goes four-on-two versus the second team (B).
2. The second team (B) has two players at half-court outside the sideline who then step on the court and play defense as the ball crosses half-court (to become four-on-four). (See diagram 1.)
3. Team B then rebounds a miss (or takes it out of bounds after a made shot) and goes four-on-two against the third team (C), who has stepped on at the opposite end of the court (see diagram 2).
4. Teams start with only two defending, and two more can enter the court once the ball passes half-court.

Coaching Points
- Play poised in a very fast-paced game.
- Look for a numerical advantage, then play controlled four-on-four.
- Winners don't have to run sprints at the end.

Variations
- Add defensive pressure before the ball crosses half-court and on the inbounds pass.
- Add a theme (e.g., the offense must pass to the post player at least once).

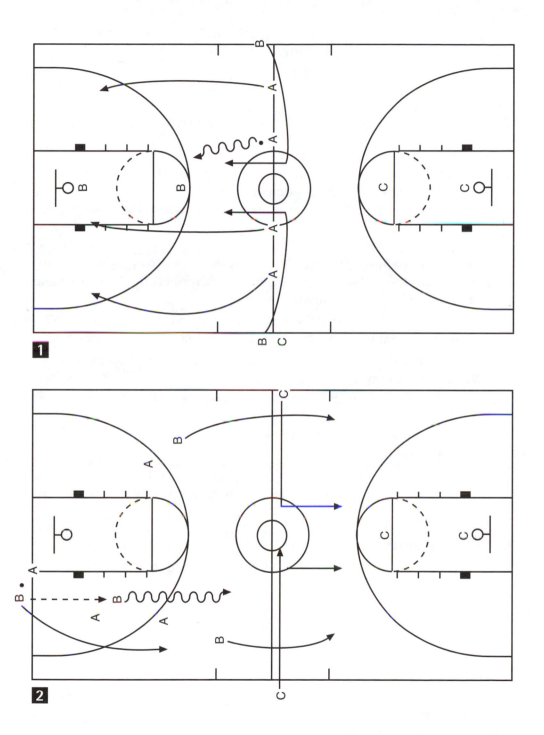

Tap Drill

Coach Bill Gibbons
School Holy Cross College

Purpose
To work on securing loose balls and speed dribbling while not under pursuit.

Organization
One player is placed downcourt at the free throw line; the others go in two lines on the baseline (one line is offensive and the other is defensive). The coach stands with one ball at the free throw line closer to the baseline.

Procedure
1. On the first whistle, the first player in the offensive line (O_1) sprints to pick up the ball at the free throw line (dropped by the coach) and starts speed dribbling down the court.
2. On the second whistle, the first player in the defensive line (X_1) sprints to tap the ball away to her teammate (X_2). (See diagram 1.)
3. X_2 is ready to secure a tapped ball, and she keeps her head up to avoid the offensive player running at her.
4. X_1 taps the ball away and then changes direction to look for a pass from X_2.
5. After receiving the pass, X_1 makes a strong layup and X_2 sprints to get the rebound before it hits the floor.
6. X_2 outlets the ball to the coach and the next two in line go on the next whistle. O_1 remains down at the opposite free throw line to become the new X_2. (See diagram 2.)

Coaching Points
- Players should pick up loose balls with two hands and keep their heads up when speed dribbling downcourt.
- All players should sprint back through the play.
- Be ready for loose balls and secure them; avoid the opponent and make a good pass for an easy two points, then sprint to follow up.

Variation
A good variation is to hit X_1 directly; she can fan out to the wing position (as if no one is going to the hoop) and wait to hit the trailer (X_2) with a chest pass for a jumper. Both players go to the boards hard and finish the play if the shot is missed. Players should change lines, work on dribbling with the other hand, and look to tap the ball away.

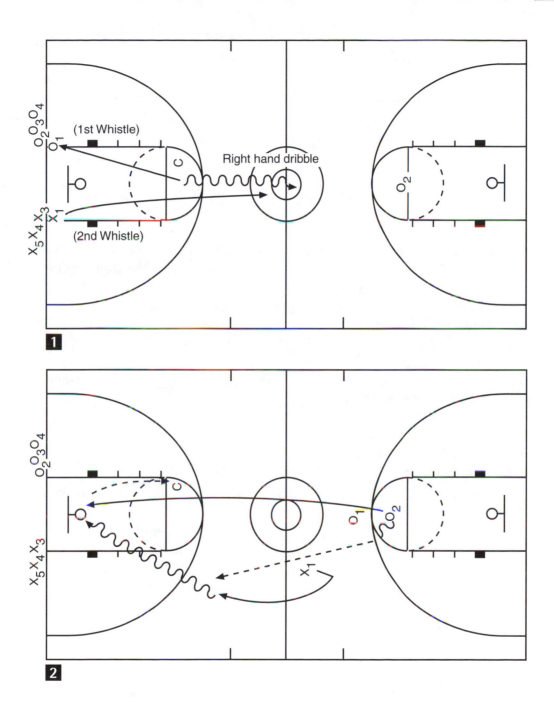

1

$O_2 O_3 O_4$

O_1 (1st Whistle)

C

Right hand dribble

$X_5 X_4 X_3 X_1$

(2nd Whistle)

O_2

2

$O_2 O_3 O_4$

C

$X_5 X_4 X_3$

O_1 O_2

X_1

Three-Player Break

Coach Joan Bonvicini
School University of Arizona

Purpose

To teach players to fill all three lanes as quickly as possible. This drill will give players options to run in a three-player break situation.

Organization

The entire team lines up in three lines on the baseline. The center line has a ball.

Procedure

1. Players are in three lines underneath the basket at the baseline. Every group of three should have at least one post player. The middle line players should all have a ball.

2. The first three players step out with the middle player (with the ball) under the basket and the two wings at the elbows of the key.

3. The player with the ball tosses it off the backboard and rebounds yelling "ball." The other two players sprint to the sidelines calling "outlet." The rebounder overhead passes to one of the wings and then fills the lane opposite her pass (diagram 1).

4. The opposite wing sprints to the middle of the floor yelling "middle." The outlet now chest passes to the middle player, who dribbles upcourt. Both wings are wide, calling their lanes either "right" or "left."

5. The player with the ball jump stops outside the key and bounce passes to one of the wings for a layup. The other wing rebounds if the shot is missed (diagram 2).

6. Once the shot is made, the players step off and the next three players in line begin the same drill. The drill continues until all groups of three have shot a layup.

7. Once all groups have done the drill the coach can now add options. For example
   a. a bounce pass for a layup;
   b. a jump shot from the wing with a rebounder putting up a shot if the wing misses; or
   c. a pass back to the top where the middle player jump stops at the top of the key and passes to the wing, who fakes away and steps back to the ball for a jumper at the top (both wings should rebound).

Coaching Points

- Players can switch lines so guards will rebound and posts will fill the lanes.
- Call out lanes when running and run as wide as possible.
- Use cones to ensure that players run wide in the lanes.
- Use coaches at the top of the key to force jump stops outside the lane.
- Players should run the fast break as quickly as possible without hurrying or being out of control.

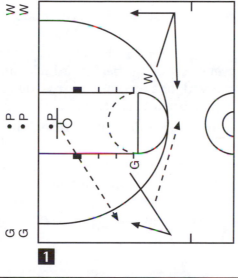

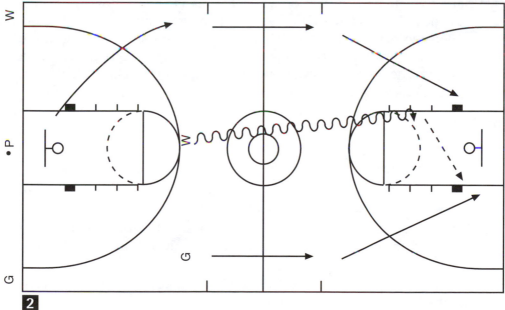

Three-on-Two-on-One Break

Coach Joan Bonvicini
School University of Arizona

Purpose
To teach a live fast break with an advantage to the offense. Players learn to read defenses, and the defense learns to force jump shots and prevent layups.

Organization
Two players line up at the half-court sideline on opposite sides. The rest of the team is in three lines on a baseline. The middle line has a ball.

Procedure
1. Run a three-player break off the backboard with an outlet pass. As the ball hits the backboard for a rebound, the two defenders come into the center circle and then backpedal playing tandem defense (diagram 1).

2. The three players on offense fill the three lanes with the ball, advancing up the middle.

3. Once the ball crosses half-court, there should be no more than three passes by the offense before a shot is attempted.

4. If a basket is made in the three-on-two situation, the shooter for example O_1, becomes the defensive player (X_1) and the defense takes the ball out on the baseline.

5. Once a shot is attempted, all players should rebound. If the defense gets the rebound, the person who attempted the first shot sprints back to the other end for defense. The two defensive players become offensive players, and the drill is now a two-on-one situation going the other way. The two offensive players now become defensive players and wait for a new group at the half-court sideline (diagram 2).

6. Players proceed in a two-on-one and attempt to score.

Coaching Points
- Defenders in a three-on-two situation should be in a tandem defense. The top player stops the ball, and the bottom player defends the first pass.

- Players on offense in a three-on-two situation should move the ball quickly for a solid jumper or layup.

- Players on offense in a two-on-one situation should pass the ball quickly back and forth to force the defense to commit to them. They should always score on a layup.

- The defense in a two-on-one situation should fake at the offensive player and try to force them into a jump shot.

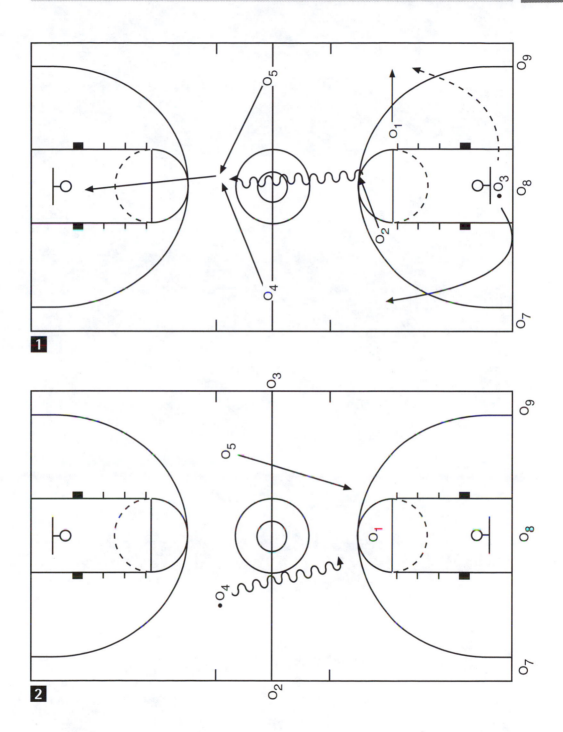

1

2

SITUATION DRILLS

Who could forget the last-second shot that gave North Carolina the NCAA title in 1995? Has there been a more dramatic finish to an NCAA title game since then—or ever? Special situations are more than tricks up the coach's sleeve. Successful special situation plays are clearly communicated, practiced often, and part of a team's repertoire of scoring options. The chance of performing well in a special situation is directly related to how you prepare your team for the climate and conditions they will likely face.

Veteran coaches share a few of their best secrets in this chapter. Notice the common thread in their situations—keep it simple. The stress level is usually high, time is a factor, and the number and quality of players remaining to perform in the situation is likely to be compromised. And whatever you do, share and practice your play and plan. It is not likely to do your team much good at the heat of the moment if the players are not sure what to do!

"Special"

Coach Mary Hile-Nepfel
School University of San Francisco

Purpose
To set up a last-second shot.

Organization
Five players and one ball.

Procedure
1. The point guard must drive the ball toward the elbow, opposite the (P) post player.
2. Your best shooter, for example O_2, will set a crossscreen for the post player then pop to the elbow.
3. The point guard has four options: (1) shoot the ball, (2) pass to the post player, (3) pass to the player at the elbow (O_3), or (4) pass to the player in the corner (O_4).

Coaching Points
The point guard must read the defense to make the appropriate pass. Leave enough time on the clock to get an offensive rebound and putback.

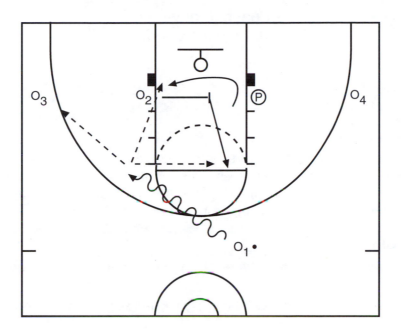

Quick Shot

Coach Cindy Stein
School University of Missouri

Purpose
To score off an inbound set.

Organization
Player O_1 is the best passer and second-best shooter; she has the ball out of bounds. Player O_2 is the best shooter and perimeter driver. Player O_3 is a solid screener and inside player. Player O_4 is the third-best shooter with some range. Player O_5 is the biggest post player (see the play setup).

Procedure
1. Player O_2 cuts off the players' O_3 and O_5 doublescreen for a quick shot or drive (diagram 1).
2. Player O_3 cuts off the O_4 player's backside screen for a second option shot (diagram 2).
3. Player O_1 comes off the player O_3's screen for a reverse pass from player O_4 (see diagram 3).

Coaching Points
- Timing on screens, cuts, and ball fakes is critical.
- Put players in positions in which they have the skill to help the play succeed.
- Practice it from both sides of the floor.

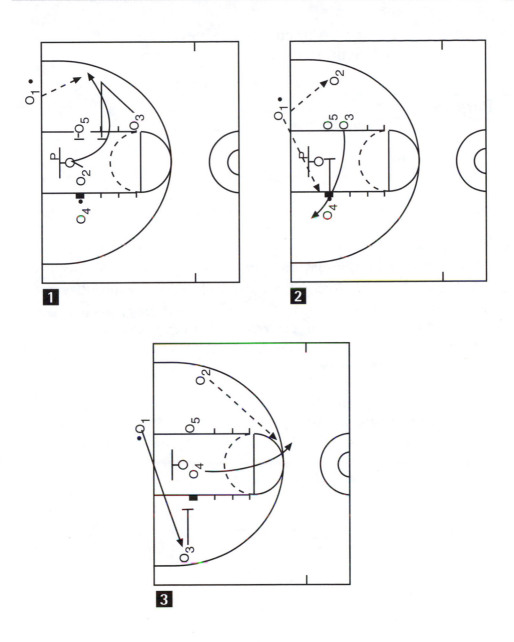

Long Shot

Coach Cindy Stein
School University of Missouri

Purpose
To score at the opposite end with little time remaining.

Organization
Player O_1 is the best ballhandler and penetrator. Player O_2 is the fastest athlete and a good shooter. Player O_3 acts as a wing. Player O_4 has a strong arm and quick speed. Player O_5 is the biggest post player (see diagram).

Procedure
1. Player O_4 looks for players O_2 or O_3 going off backside screens.
2. Player O_1 rolls to receive the ball and dribbles upcourt (diagram 1).
3. Player O_2 runs off player O_3's baseline screen while player O_4 sprints down the floor to go off player O_5's backside screen (diagram 2).
4. Player O_1 then has the option of hitting O_2, O_3, O_4, or O_5 who are all rolling or cutting to receive the pass.

Coaching Points
- Speed and hustle make this play successful.
- Good, solid, and legal screens; defenders may be blindsided. Be prepared for contact.
- Get a shot off before clock expires; give yourself a chance to score.

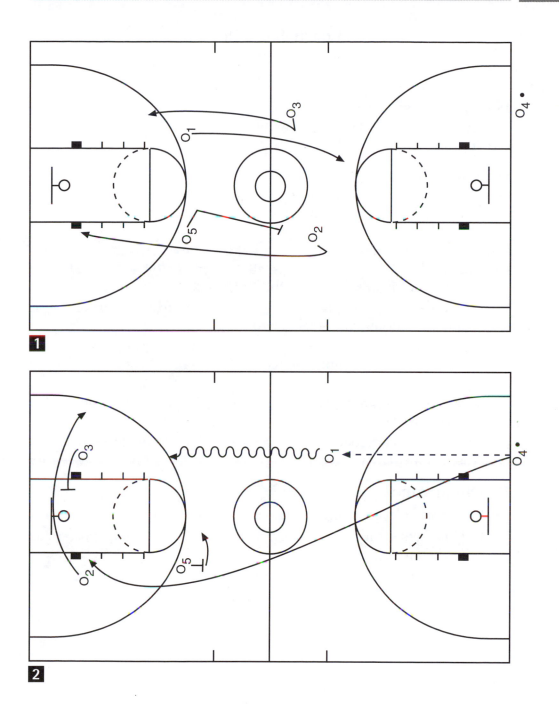

1

2

Two-Minute Drill

Coach Sonja Hogg
School Baylor University

Purpose

To teach players to handle late-game situations when the score is close. Focus on execution.

Organization

Ten players and one ball; use the full court.

Procedure

1. There are two minutes on the game clock. The coaches tell their teams the score and how much time is left. *Example:* gold team 72 and green team 76. It's gold's ball out in the back court.

2. Scrimmage from this point. Designate timeouts to each team. *Example:* gold team one and green team two.

3. The coaches set up foul situations for each team. *Example:* gold team isn't in one and one until the second foul, while the green team is in the one and one.

4. When timeouts are called, focus on having the players do exactly what they're told to do.

5. If players do not follow instructions, stop the scrimmage and correct them immediately.

Coaching Points

- Emphasize players doing exactly as instructed during timeouts.
- Help players learn game strategy, such as when to maintain possession and when to foul.
- Focus on mental control in pressure situations.

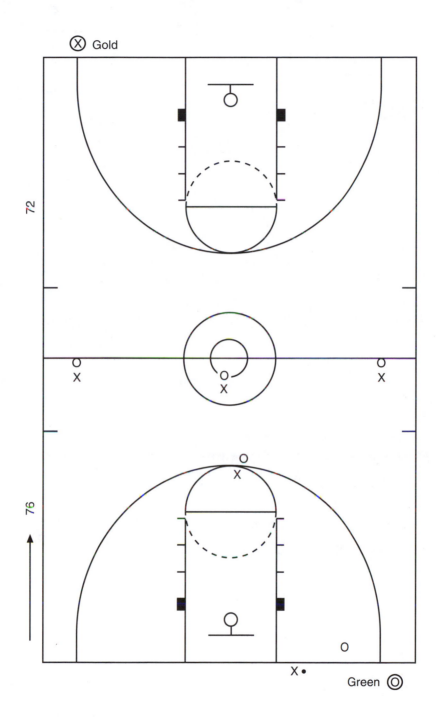

ABOUT THE WBCA

Founded in 1981, the Women's Basketball Coaches Association (WBCA) is the largest such organization in the United States. Its mission is to promote women's basketball by unifying coaches at all levels to develop a reputable identity for the sport of women's basketball and to foster and promote the development of the game in all of its aspects as an amateur sport for women and girls.

The WBCA is involved in several events and clinics throughout the year, including: the High School All-America Game (televised on ESPN2), the three-day educational Coaches' Academy, WBCA Premier Basketball Camps, the WBCA All-Star Challenge, the Coaches vs. Cancer Challenge, Coaching Clinics across the nation, and Sears Collegiate Champions (SCC) program. Through these events the WBCA not only tries to highlight exceptional talent among women and girl players but also provide opportunities for coaches at all levels to better themselves.

In addition to the activities that the WBCA puts on and sponsors, they have an extensive awards program through which the best, brightest, and most talented athletes, coaches, and contributors to women's basketball are honored. There is also the annual WBCA National Convention held in conjunction with the NCAA Women's Final Four and their three publications (Coaching Women's Basketball, At the Buzzer, and Fastbreak Alert) which provide coverage on all aspects of women's basketball from high school to professional.

For more details on these and the many activities and opportunities available from the WBCA, check out their Web site at: www.wbca.org.

The following are coaches who contributed drills to *WBCA's Offensive Basketball Drills*:

- Joan Bonvicini, University of Arizona
- Jody Conradt, University of Texas
- Jim Davis, Clemson University
- Kathy Delaney-Smith, Harvard University
- Nancy Fahey, Washington University
- Mike Geary, Northern Michigan University
- Bill Gibbons, Holy Cross College
- Chris Gobrecht, University of Southern California
- Theresa Grentz, University of Illinois
- Sue Gunter, Louisiana State University
- Mary Hile-Nepfel, University of San Francisco
- Sonja Hogg, Baylor University
- Patrick Knapp, Georgetown University
- Wendy Larry, Old Dominion University
- Angie Lee, University of Iowa
- Bob Lindsay, Kent State
- Bernadette Mattox, University of Kentucky
- Muffet McGraw, University of Notre Dame
- Joe McKeown, George Washington University
- Trina Patterson, College of William and Mary
- Rene Portland, Penn State University
- Gordy Presnell, Seattle Pacific University
- Carol Ross, University of Florida
- Jody Runge, University of Oregon
- Debbie Ryan, University of Virginia
- Paul Sanderford, University of Nebraska
- David Smith, Bellarman College
- Cindy Stein, University of Missouri
- Barbara Stevens, Bentley College
- Pat Summitt, University of Tennessee
- Tara VanDerveer, Stanford University
- Marian Washington, University of Kansas
- Kay Yow, North Carolina State

Play defense, run transition, and practice like a champion

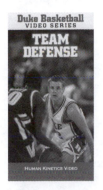

Duke is known for its tough team defense, and four Blue Devils have been chosen Defensive Player of the Year during Coach Mike Kryzewski's tenure. *Team Defense* shows how you can transform five individual players into a single, basket-denying unit. This tape is a complete clinic on the techniques required to fulfill individual position responsibilities and the tactical adjustments required to stop offensive attacks of all kinds.

(46-minute videotape)
1999 • Item MHKV0190 • ISBN 0-7360-0190-5
$29.95 ($44.95 Canadian)

Duke's emphasis on beating their opponent in switching from defense to offense and from offense to defense has now become a hallmark of their success. *Transition Game* shows that this advantage is developed on the practice court by design, drilling, and desire, and it describes how you can achieve this advantage for yourself or your team.

(52-minute videotape)
1999 • Item MHKV0192 • ISBN 0-7360-0192-1
$29.95 ($44.95 Canadian)

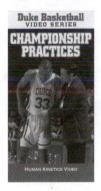

Championship Practices provides a unique behind-the-scenes look at how Coach K and his staff plan and conduct their practice sessions to produce powerhouse teams. From season objectives to specific player teaching points, this video shows how you can transfer the blueprint for success to players. Coach K teaches, corrects, reinforces, and attends to all aspects of the game in his classroom on the court.

(37-minute videotape)
1999 • Item MHKV0195 • ISBN 0-7360-0195-6
$29.95 ($44.95 Canadian)

Special Package Price

All three Duke videos
Item MHKV0241 • ISBN 0-7360-0241-3 • $79.95 ($119.95 Canadian)

Visit the Human Kinetics Web site at
www.humankinetics.com

Tools to take your game to a higher level

In the *Basketball for Women* book, authors Nancy Lieberman-Cline and ESPN/ABC Sports anchor Robin Roberts provide

• 111 offensive and defensive drills
• conditioning programs and guidelines
• ways to maximize practice game performance, and
• tips for handling the recruitment process.

1995 • Paperback • 296 pp • Item PLIE0610
ISBN 0-87322-610-0 • $16.95 ($24.95 Canadian)

Basketball for Women: Offensive Skills shows players how to become offensive triple threats—to pass, dribble, or shoot. Lieberman-Cline provides instruction and drills for developing moves without the ball, improving ball-handling skills, sharpening shooting technique, and making better decisions about attacking the basket.

(48-minute videotape)
1998 • Item MLIE0987 • ISBN 0-88011-987-X
$24.95 ($36.95 Canadian)

Basketball for Women: Defense and Rebounding teaches the finer points of shutting down the opponent and banging the boards. The tape provides instruction and drills for pressuring the ball, denying the pass, taking charges, positioning for rebounds, and much, much more.

(25-minute videotape)
1998 • Item MLIE0991 • ISBN 0-88011-991-8
$24.95 ($36.95 Canadian)

Special Package Prices

Basketball for Women two-video set
Item MLIE0992 • ISBN 0-88011-992-6 • $39.95 ($59.95 Canadian)
Basketball for Women book plus two-video set
Item MLIE0995 • ISBN 0-88011-995-0 • $54.95 ($82.50 Canadian)

To place your order, U.S. customers call TOLL FREE

1-800-747-4457

Customers outside the U.S. place your order using the appropriate telephone
number/address shown in the front of this book.

Human Kinetics
The Premier Publisher for Sports & Fitness
P.O. Box 5076, Champaign, IL 61825-5076

Prices are subject to change.